OpenID Connect

James Relington

DEDICATION

This book is dedicated to all the professionals working tirelessly to secure digital identities and protect organizations from ever-evolving threats. To the cybersecurity teams, IT administrators, and identity management experts who ensure safe and seamless access for users—your work is invaluable. And to my family and friends, whose support and encouragement made this journey possible, thank you.

AKNOWLEDGEMENTS

I would like to express my deepest gratitude to everyone who contributed to the creation of this book. To my colleagues and mentors in the cybersecurity and identity management field, your insights and expertise have been invaluable. To the organizations and professionals who shared their experiences and best practices, your contributions have enriched this work. A special thanks to my family and friends for their unwavering support and encouragement throughout this journey. Finally, to the readers, thank you for your interest in identity lifecycle management—may this book help you navigate the evolving landscape of digital security with confidence.

Introduction to OpenID Connect (OIDC)

OpenID Connect (OIDC) is a modern authentication protocol built on top of the OAuth 2.0 framework. It introduces a standardized way to verify the identity of users based on the authentication performed by an authorization server. While OAuth 2.0 was originally designed for authorization, allowing applications to access user resources without exposing their credentials, OIDC extends this capability by adding an identity layer, enabling secure and reliable authentication.

The evolution of digital services and the proliferation of online platforms have made secure identity management a cornerstone of modern web applications. Traditionally, authentication was managed through standalone systems with user credentials stored in isolated databases. This approach, however, presented challenges such as password fatigue, security vulnerabilities, and poor user experience. OpenID Connect addresses these issues by providing a unified, federated identity solution that enhances security and simplifies user authentication across multiple applications.

One of the key components of OIDC is the ID token, a JSON Web Token (JWT) that contains information about the user, known as claims. These claims can include details like the user's unique identifier, name, email address, and other profile information. The ID token allows client applications to confirm the identity of the user without needing to directly handle their credentials. This token-based approach not only improves security but also facilitates seamless integration between applications and identity providers.

In addition to ID tokens, OIDC relies on OAuth 2.0 access tokens to authorize access to user resources. While access tokens grant permission to access APIs and protected data, the ID token specifically serves to authenticate the user. This dual-token mechanism ensures that applications can both verify user identities and request access to necessary resources without compromising security.

OIDC introduces several important roles in its architecture. The End-User is the individual who wants to access a service. The Relying Party (RP), often referred to as the client, is the application that needs to authenticate the user. The OpenID Provider (OP) is the server that authenticates the user and issues tokens. This clear division of roles facilitates a streamlined authentication process, where users can log in once through an OpenID Provider and gain access to multiple relying parties without repeated logins.

A crucial feature of OIDC is its support for Single Sign-On (SSO). SSO allows users to authenticate once with an OpenID Provider and then access multiple applications without needing to log in again. This enhances the user experience by reducing the need for multiple passwords and logins, while also improving security by centralizing authentication management. OIDC's standardized approach to SSO has made it a preferred choice for many enterprises and service providers seeking to simplify user access across various platforms.

OIDC also emphasizes security and privacy. It uses strong encryption methods and secure communication protocols to protect user data. The use of JWTs ensures that tokens are tamper-proof and verifiable. Additionally, OIDC includes mechanisms like nonce and state parameters to prevent common security threats such as replay attacks and cross-site request forgery (CSRF). By adhering to robust security standards, OIDC helps organizations safeguard sensitive user information and maintain trust in their authentication processes.

The protocol supports multiple authentication flows, catering to different types of applications and use cases. The Authorization Code Flow is the most commonly used, suitable for server-side applications where tokens are exchanged securely on the backend. The Implicit Flow is designed for browser-based applications, although its use is declining due to security concerns. The Hybrid Flow combines elements of both, providing flexibility for complex scenarios. Each flow balances security and usability, allowing developers to choose the most appropriate method for their application architecture.

Another significant advantage of OIDC is its interoperability. As an open standard, OIDC is widely supported by a broad range of identity providers, including major technology companies like Google, Microsoft, and Amazon. This broad support allows developers to integrate authentication services into their applications with minimal effort, leveraging existing infrastructure and best practices. The protocol's compatibility with OAuth 2.0 also ensures that applications can easily transition from authorization-only solutions to full-fledged authentication systems.

OIDC's extensibility further contributes to its popularity. The protocol allows for custom claims and scopes, enabling organizations to tailor authentication processes to their specific needs. Developers can request specific pieces of user information by defining scopes, such as openid, profile, email, and address. This flexibility makes OIDC suitable for a wide range of applications, from simple web apps to complex enterprise systems with diverse authentication requirements.

Beyond its technical capabilities, OIDC has played a pivotal role in shaping the broader landscape of digital identity management. It has facilitated the rise of federated identity systems, where a single identity provider can serve multiple organizations and applications. This model reduces the administrative burden of managing separate user accounts while enhancing security through centralized oversight. OIDC's influence is evident in various sectors, from finance and healthcare to education and government services, where secure, reliable identity verification is critical.

Despite its strengths, implementing OIDC is not without challenges. Developers must ensure proper configuration and handling of tokens to avoid security pitfalls. Mismanagement of tokens, such as storing them insecurely or failing to validate them correctly, can expose applications to vulnerabilities. Therefore, understanding the protocol's nuances and following best practices is essential for a secure and effective implementation.

In summary, OpenID Connect represents a significant advancement in the realm of authentication protocols. By building on the robust foundation of OAuth 2.0, it provides a secure, flexible, and user-friendly solution for identity verification. Its widespread adoption, support for single sign-on, and emphasis on security make it a cornerstone of modern digital identity management. As online services continue to evolve, OIDC will remain a vital tool in ensuring secure, seamless access to applications and resources across the digital landscape.

Understanding Identity, Authentication, and Authorization

In today's interconnected digital world, the concepts of identity, authentication, and authorization are central to ensuring secure access to systems and data. While these terms are often used interchangeably, they represent distinct components within the broader realm of security and access management. Understanding how they interact is essential for anyone involved in developing, managing, or securing digital systems.

Identity is the foundation of any access control system. It refers to the set of attributes or characteristics that uniquely define an individual or entity within a system. In the digital context, identity is often represented by a username, an email address, or another unique identifier that links an individual to their digital persona. However, identity goes beyond just a simple identifier; it includes a collection of attributes such as name, role, contact information, and other personal or organizational data that describe who the user is. The accurate management of identity information is critical because it forms the basis upon which authentication and authorization decisions are made.

Authentication builds upon identity by verifying that an individual or entity is indeed who they claim to be. It is the process of proving one's identity to a system. This is typically achieved through credentials like passwords, biometric data (such as fingerprints or facial recognition), security tokens, or multi-factor authentication (MFA) methods that combine several forms of verification. For example, when a user logs into an online banking application, entering a correct username and password serves as a basic form of authentication. Adding an additional step, such as a one-time code sent to a mobile device, enhances security by ensuring that the person accessing the account possesses both knowledge (the password) and something they own (the mobile device).

While authentication establishes identity, authorization determines what actions or resources an authenticated user is allowed to access. Authorization is the process of granting or denying permissions based on the authenticated user's role, attributes, or other criteria. For instance, in an enterprise system, an authenticated employee might have access to general company resources but be restricted from viewing sensitive financial data unless they belong to the finance department. Authorization mechanisms ensure that users can only perform actions and access data that align with their permissions, thereby protecting sensitive information from unauthorized access.

The distinction between authentication and authorization is crucial. A user can be authenticated without being authorized to perform certain actions. For example, a person may successfully log into a corporate network (authentication) but still be restricted from accessing specific files or applications (authorization). Conversely, authorization cannot occur without authentication, as the system needs to know who the user is before assigning permissions.

Identity, authentication, and authorization are often managed together within frameworks known as Identity and Access Management (IAM) systems. These systems provide centralized control over user identities, authentication processes, and authorization policies, simplifying the management of access across diverse applications and platforms. IAM solutions help organizations enforce security policies, ensure compliance with regulatory requirements, and protect against unauthorized access by maintaining consistent and secure identity management practices.

In modern computing environments, especially in the context of cloud services and distributed applications, these concepts have become even more critical. Single Sign-On (SSO) is a prime example of how identity and authentication are leveraged to streamline user experiences. With SSO, users authenticate once and gain access to multiple applications without needing to log in repeatedly. This not only enhances convenience but also reduces the security risks associated with password fatigue and poor credential management.

Federated identity systems take this a step further by enabling identity sharing across different organizations or domains. Standards like SAML (Security Assertion Markup Language) and OpenID Connect facilitate the secure exchange of identity information between trusted parties, allowing users to access external services using their primary organizational credentials. This is particularly useful in scenarios where collaboration across different entities is required, such as in partnerships between companies or in educational institutions providing access to third-party tools.

As technology continues to evolve, so do the methods of authentication and authorization. Biometric authentication, which uses unique physical characteristics like fingerprints, iris patterns, or facial recognition, has gained widespread adoption due to its convenience and security. Similarly, behavioral biometrics, which analyze patterns like typing speed or mouse movements, are emerging as innovative ways to continuously authenticate users without interrupting their workflow.

On the authorization front, more granular and dynamic models are being developed to adapt to complex security needs. Role-Based Access Control (RBAC) has been a traditional approach, where permissions are assigned based on predefined roles within an organization. However, Attribute-Based Access Control (ABAC) is gaining traction as it offers more flexibility by granting access based on a combination of user attributes, environmental conditions, and resource characteristics. This allows for more fine-tuned control over who can access what, under specific circumstances.

Understanding the interplay between identity, authentication, and authorization is essential for building secure systems and protecting sensitive information. These concepts not only safeguard digital resources but also shape the user experience, influencing how individuals interact with technology in their personal and professional lives. As security threats continue to evolve, the principles of identity, authentication, and authorization will remain at the forefront of digital defense strategies, ensuring that only the right people have access to the right resources at the right time.

Key Concepts and Terminology

OpenID Connect (OIDC) is a modern authentication protocol built on top of the OAuth 2.0 framework, providing a standardized way to verify user identities and obtain basic profile information in a secure manner. To fully grasp how OIDC functions, it's important to understand the key concepts and terminology that form its foundation. This chapter delves into the essential components, actors, and processes that make OIDC a reliable and widely adopted identity layer in today's digital ecosystem.

At its core, OIDC extends OAuth 2.0, which was primarily designed for delegated authorization. OAuth 2.0 allows applications to access resources on behalf of a user without directly handling their credentials. However, OAuth 2.0 does not provide a mechanism to authenticate users or verify their identities. This is where OIDC steps in, introducing an identity layer that allows clients to confirm who the user is, alongside gaining access to protected resources. Understanding this distinction between authorization and authentication is vital, as it clarifies why OIDC was developed and how it complements OAuth 2.0.

A foundational term in OIDC is the Identity Provider (IdP). The Identity Provider is the entity responsible for authenticating users and issuing identity tokens. These tokens contain information about the authenticated user, known as claims, which are used by client applications to establish user identity. Examples of popular Identity Providers include Google, Microsoft, and Okta. When a user logs into an application using their Google account, Google acts as the Identity Provider, verifying the user's identity and providing the necessary credentials to the requesting application.

Another critical concept is the Relying Party (RP), also known as the client. This is the application or service that relies on the Identity Provider to authenticate users. The Relying Party initiates the authentication request and, upon receiving the identity token from the IdP, uses the information within it to log the user into the system. The Relying Party does not handle user credentials directly, which enhances security by minimizing the exposure of sensitive information.

The End-User is the individual who interacts with the Relying Party and whose identity is being authenticated. The end-user initiates the authentication process, typically by logging into an application using their credentials from an Identity Provider. In OIDC, the end-user experience is streamlined, often allowing for single sign-on (SSO) capabilities where users can access multiple applications with a single set of credentials.

A key technical component of OIDC is the ID Token. Unlike OAuth 2.0's access tokens, which are intended for authorization, the ID Token is specifically designed for authentication purposes. It is a JSON Web Token (JWT) that contains claims about the user, such as their unique identifier (sub), name, email address, and other profile information. The ID Token is digitally signed by the Identity Provider, ensuring its integrity and authenticity. Client applications validate the ID Token to confirm the identity of the end-user.

Access Tokens also play a role in OIDC, though their primary function remains consistent with OAuth 2.0. These tokens grant client applications access to protected resources on behalf of the user. While access tokens can contain some user information, they are not intended for authentication and should not be used to verify user identity. This distinction underscores the importance of using ID Tokens for authentication and access tokens for resource authorization.

Another important term is Claims, which are pieces of information about the user included in the ID Token. Claims can be standard, such as sub (subject identifier), name, email, and iat (issued at time), or custom, depending on the requirements of the application. Claims provide the necessary data for the Relying Party to understand who the user is and tailor the user experience accordingly.

The Authorization Endpoint and Token Endpoint are critical URLs in the OIDC protocol flow. The Authorization Endpoint is where the end-user is redirected to authenticate with the Identity Provider. After successful authentication, the Identity Provider redirects the user back to the Relying Party with an authorization code. This code is then exchanged at the Token Endpoint for an ID Token and, optionally, an access token. This two-step process enhances security by ensuring that tokens are transmitted directly between servers, reducing the risk of interception.

Scopes are another fundamental concept in OIDC. Scopes define the level of access requested by the client application. In OIDC, the openid scope is mandatory and signifies that the request is for authentication purposes. Additional scopes, such as profile, email, and address, can be included to request specific pieces of user information. The use of scopes allows for granular control over what information is shared with the client application, giving users more transparency and control over their data.

Discovery and Dynamic Client Registration are advanced features of OIDC that enhance its flexibility and ease of integration. Discovery allows client applications to automatically obtain configuration information about the Identity Provider, such as endpoint URLs and supported features, through a well-known URL (.well-known/openid-configuration). Dynamic Client Registration enables clients to register with the Identity Provider programmatically, reducing manual configuration and streamlining the setup process.

Session Management is also a crucial aspect of OIDC. It deals with maintaining and terminating user sessions across different applications and devices. OIDC provides mechanisms for single sign-on (SSO) and single logout (SLO), allowing users to log in once and access multiple applications or log out from one application and be signed out from all connected services. This capability is essential for enhancing user convenience and security in multi-application environments.

Finally, Proof Key for Code Exchange (PKCE) is a security extension to the Authorization Code flow, designed to mitigate certain attack vectors, such as authorization code interception. PKCE is especially important for public clients, like mobile and single-page applications, that cannot securely store client secrets. By introducing an additional layer of verification, PKCE enhances the overall security of the OIDC authentication process.

Understanding these key concepts and terminologies is essential for effectively implementing and utilizing OpenID Connect. By building on the robust framework of OAuth 2.0 and introducing critical identity management capabilities, OIDC has become a cornerstone of modern authentication and authorization systems. As digital applications continue to proliferate, the importance of secure, user-friendly identity solutions like OIDC will only grow, underscoring the value of mastering its foundational principles.

Components of the OIDC Protocol

OpenID Connect (OIDC) is an authentication protocol built on top of the OAuth 2.0 framework. It introduces a standardized layer for verifying user identities while maintaining OAuth's robust authorization features. To fully understand how OIDC operates and why it has become a preferred standard in modern identity management systems, it is essential to explore its key components. These elements work together to ensure secure, seamless authentication and authorization across different applications and platforms.

At the heart of OIDC lies the Identity Provider (IdP). The Identity Provider is responsible for authenticating users and issuing tokens that contain verified identity information. When a user attempts to log into an application, the IdP handles the authentication process—whether through passwords, biometrics, or multi-factor authentication methods—and then generates tokens to convey this information securely to the requesting application. Examples of common Identity Providers include Google, Microsoft Azure Active Directory, and Okta. The IdP plays a crucial role in centralizing authentication, enabling Single Sign-On (SSO) and reducing the need for multiple credential sets across different services.

The Relying Party (RP), also known as the client, is the application or service that relies on the Identity Provider to authenticate users. The RP initiates authentication requests and processes the identity information received from the IdP. This setup allows applications to offload the complexities of user authentication to trusted Identity Providers, focusing instead on delivering core services. For instance, when a user logs into a third-party application using their Google account, that application functions as the Relying Party, depending on Google to verify the user's identity and provide the necessary credentials.

The End-User is the individual whose identity is being authenticated. The user interacts with both the Relying Party and the Identity

Provider during the authentication process. For the end-user, OIDC streamlines the login experience, often allowing access to multiple applications using a single set of credentials through Single Sign-On. This not only simplifies the user experience but also enhances security by minimizing the need to manage multiple passwords.

A central technical element of the OIDC protocol is the ID Token. This is a JSON Web Token (JWT) that contains claims about the user, such as their unique identifier (sub), name, email address, and other relevant profile information. The ID Token is digitally signed by the Identity Provider to ensure its authenticity and integrity. Unlike access tokens used in OAuth 2.0, which grant permission to access protected resources, the ID Token is specifically designed for verifying the user's identity. The Relying Party validates this token to confirm that the authentication was successful and that the user is who they claim to be.

In addition to the ID Token, OIDC uses Access Tokens and Refresh Tokens. The Access Token allows the Relying Party to access specific resources on behalf of the user, such as APIs or user data stored on the server. This token is typically short-lived to reduce security risks. The Refresh Token, on the other hand, is used to obtain new Access Tokens without requiring the user to re-authenticate. This token has a longer lifespan and is securely stored to maintain session continuity in applications.

OIDC relies on specific endpoints to manage the flow of information between the Relying Party and the Identity Provider. The Authorization Endpoint is where the Relying Party redirects the user to initiate authentication. After the user successfully logs in, they are redirected back to the application with an authorization code. This code is then exchanged at the Token Endpoint for an ID Token, Access Token, and optionally, a Refresh Token. The UserInfo Endpoint allows the Relying Party to retrieve additional profile information about the user, provided the necessary scopes were granted during the authentication process.

Another crucial concept in OIDC is Scopes. Scopes define the level of access requested by the Relying Party. The mandatory openid scope signals that the request is for authentication purposes. Additional scopes like profile, email, and address allow the application to access specific pieces of user information. This granular approach to permissions ensures that users have control over what information is shared with applications, enhancing both security and privacy.

OIDC also supports Discovery and Dynamic Client Registration. Discovery simplifies the configuration process by allowing Relying Parties to automatically retrieve information about the Identity Provider, such as endpoint URLs and supported features, through a well-known URL (.well-known/openid-configuration). Dynamic Client Registration enables applications to register with the Identity Provider programmatically, reducing the need for manual configuration and making it easier to integrate new applications into an existing identity infrastructure.

Security is a cornerstone of the OIDC protocol. It incorporates features like nonce and state parameters to prevent common attacks such as replay attacks and cross-site request forgery (CSRF). The Proof Key for Code Exchange (PKCE) extension adds an additional layer of security, particularly for public clients like mobile and single-page applications that cannot securely store client secrets. PKCE ensures that the authorization code exchanged between the Relying Party and the Identity Provider has not been intercepted or altered.

Finally, OIDC addresses session management and logout processes to provide a consistent user experience across different applications. Single Sign-On (SSO) allows users to authenticate once and gain access to multiple services without re-entering credentials. Conversely, Single Logout (SLO) ensures that logging out from one application terminates the session across all connected applications, maintaining security and session integrity.

By combining these components—Identity Providers, Relying Parties, tokens, scopes, endpoints, and robust security measures—OIDC offers a comprehensive solution for secure and user-friendly authentication. Its widespread adoption across industries underscores its effectiveness in addressing modern identity management challenges, from simplifying user experiences to safeguarding sensitive data. Understanding these components is essential for anyone looking to implement or manage OIDC in their applications.

The Role of the Authorization Server

In the realm of modern authentication and authorization protocols, the authorization server plays a pivotal role in ensuring secure access to resources and managing user identities. Within the OpenID Connect (OIDC) and OAuth 2.0 frameworks, the authorization server serves as the central authority responsible for issuing tokens, authenticating users, and enforcing security policies. Its functionality is essential for enabling seamless, secure communication between clients, resource servers, and identity providers.

At its core, the authorization server is tasked with the issuance of tokens that grant clients access to protected resources. These tokens include access tokens, which allow clients to interact with APIs or services on behalf of the user, and ID tokens, which are unique to OIDC and carry identity information about the authenticated user. By issuing these tokens, the authorization server bridges the gap between users who own the data and the applications that need to access it, all while maintaining a secure environment where sensitive information is protected.

One of the primary responsibilities of the authorization server is user authentication. When a client application requests access to a user's resources, it redirects the user to the authorization server's authentication endpoint. Here, the user is prompted to enter their credentials, such as a username and password, or to authenticate using multi-factor authentication (MFA) methods. The authorization server verifies the user's identity, ensuring that only legitimate users can proceed. This authentication process may involve additional security measures like biometric verification or one-time passwords (OTPs), depending on the configured security policies.

After successfully authenticating the user, the authorization server proceeds to authorize the requested actions. This involves evaluating whether the authenticated user has the necessary permissions to access the requested resources. The server considers factors such as the scopes requested by the client application, the user's roles and attributes, and any predefined access control policies. If the authorization request is valid, the server issues the appropriate tokens;

otherwise, it denies the request, ensuring that unauthorized access attempts are thwarted.

Another critical function of the authorization server is token management. Once authentication and authorization are complete, the server generates and issues tokens that the client can use to access protected resources. The access token is used for resource access, while the ID token carries information about the user's identity, and the refresh token allows the client to obtain new tokens without requiring the user to re-authenticate. The authorization server ensures that these tokens are securely generated, signed, and distributed. It also enforces token expiration policies, ensuring that tokens have limited lifespans to minimize security risks.

Security is a cornerstone of the authorization server's role. It is responsible for implementing secure communication protocols such as HTTPS to protect data in transit and ensure that tokens are transmitted securely between clients and resource servers. The server also leverages cryptographic techniques to sign tokens, enabling clients and resource servers to verify their authenticity and integrity. Additionally, the authorization server employs mechanisms like Proof Key for Code Exchange (PKCE) to protect against authorization code interception attacks, especially in public clients like mobile and single-page applications.

The authorization server also plays a crucial role in user consent management. When a client application requests access to specific user data or permissions, the authorization server prompts the user to review and approve or deny the request. This consent process ensures that users maintain control over their personal information and are aware of how their data will be used. The server records the user's consent decisions and enforces them in future authorization requests, enhancing transparency and trust in the system.

In federated identity systems, the authorization server often doubles as an identity provider (IdP). In this role, it not only authenticates users and issues tokens but also manages user identities and profile information. The server maintains a user directory or connects to external identity providers to retrieve user data. By centralizing identity management, the authorization server simplifies the authentication process for both users and client applications, enabling Single Sign-On (SSO) capabilities across multiple services and domains.

The authorization endpoint and token endpoint are key components of the authorization server's architecture. The authorization endpoint is responsible for handling user authentication and consent, while the token endpoint manages the issuance of tokens after the authorization process is complete. These endpoints are critical touchpoints in the OIDC and OAuth 2.0 flows, facilitating secure communication between clients, users, and resource servers. The server also provides a userinfo endpoint in OIDC implementations, allowing clients to retrieve additional user profile information after authentication.

The authorization server must also handle session management to ensure secure user experiences. It tracks user sessions and enforces session timeouts, reducing the risk of unauthorized access due to inactive or abandoned sessions. In environments that support Single Sign-On, the authorization server manages user sessions across multiple applications, allowing users to log in once and gain access to various services without repeated authentication prompts. Conversely, Single Logout (SLO) ensures that when a user logs out from one application, they are also logged out from all connected services, enhancing security and session control.

Scalability and reliability are essential considerations for the authorization server, especially in large-scale or enterprise environments. The server must be capable of handling high volumes of authentication and authorization requests while maintaining low latency and high availability. To achieve this, authorization servers often employ load balancing, redundancy, and failover mechanisms to ensure uninterrupted service. Additionally, audit logging and monitoring are integral to the server's operation, providing visibility into authentication and authorization events and enabling the detection of anomalies or security threats.

Modern authorization servers also support dynamic client registration and discovery mechanisms to simplify integration with new applications. Dynamic client registration allows client applications to register with the authorization server programmatically, reducing the need for manual configuration. The discovery mechanism provides a standardized way for clients to obtain configuration details about the authorization server, such as supported endpoints, token formats, and security features, via a well-known URL.

The role of the authorization server extends beyond technical functions to encompass compliance with regulatory and privacy requirements. It must enforce data protection regulations, such as the General Data Protection Regulation (GDPR), by ensuring that user data is handled responsibly and that users have control over their personal information. This includes supporting features like data minimization, user consent, and the right to be forgotten, where users can request the deletion of their data from the system.

In summary, the authorization server is a cornerstone of secure authentication and authorization frameworks like OpenID Connect and OAuth 2.0. By managing user authentication, issuing tokens, enforcing security policies, and ensuring regulatory compliance, the authorization server plays a vital role in protecting sensitive data and enabling secure access to digital resources. Its ability to balance security, scalability, and user experience makes it an indispensable component of modern identity and access management systems.

The Resource Owner and Relying Party Explained

In the world of modern authentication protocols, especially within the frameworks of OAuth 2.0 and OpenID Connect (OIDC), two key entities play critical roles in the secure exchange of information: the Resource Owner and the Relying Party. Understanding these components is essential for grasping how access control and identity verification work in distributed systems. These roles facilitate the secure transfer of data while protecting user privacy and maintaining the integrity of digital resources.

The Resource Owner is typically the end-user who owns the data or resource that a third-party application wants to access. In simpler terms, the Resource Owner is the individual whose personal or sensitive information is stored on a server and who has the authority to grant or deny access to that information. For example, if you're using a mobile fitness app that needs to pull data from your Google account, you, as the user, are the Resource Owner. You control who gets access to your information, and without your explicit consent, no external application can retrieve that data.

While the Resource Owner is most commonly a human user, in some cases, it could also be a system or application. For example, in machine-to-machine communication where automated processes share data, the Resource Owner might be a specific system that manages certain data sets. Regardless of the scenario, the core idea remains the same: the Resource Owner holds the keys to access specific resources and has the ultimate say in who can interact with them.

To facilitate this process, OAuth 2.0 and OIDC introduce another essential player: the Relying Party (RP). The Relying Party, often referred to as the client, is the application or service that seeks access to the Resource Owner's data. This could be anything from a social media platform integrating your calendar to a third-party app accessing your contact list or photos. The Relying Party relies on an Authorization Server (or Identity Provider in OIDC) to authenticate the user and obtain the necessary permissions to access the data.

The interaction between the Resource Owner and the Relying Party is mediated through a process that ensures security and privacy. When the Relying Party needs access to the Resource Owner's data, it doesn't request the data directly. Instead, it redirects the Resource Owner to the Authorization Server. The Resource Owner is then presented with a consent screen, detailing the permissions being requested. This transparency is crucial, as it allows the Resource Owner to make informed decisions about what data to share and with whom.

Once the Resource Owner grants permission, the Authorization Server issues tokens that the Relying Party can use to access the requested resources. These tokens include the Access Token, which provides access to specific APIs or data, and in the case of OIDC, the ID Token, which confirms the user's identity. Importantly, the Relying Party never handles the Resource Owner's credentials directly. This separation enhances security by minimizing the risk of credential theft or misuse.

The roles of the Resource Owner and the Relying Party are further clarified when considering scopes and permissions. Scopes define the level of access that the Relying Party is requesting. For instance, an application might request read-only access to your contacts or full access to modify your calendar events. The Resource Owner reviews these scopes during the consent process and can choose to approve or deny specific permissions. This granularity ensures that the Resource Owner maintains control over their data, sharing only what is necessary for the application to function.

Another important aspect of this relationship is trust. The Resource Owner must trust both the Authorization Server and the Relying Party. Trust in the Authorization Server comes from its role as a gatekeeper, ensuring that authentication processes are secure and that sensitive information is handled responsibly. Trust in the Relying Party is built through transparent communication about how data will be used, as well as adherence to security best practices in managing tokens and accessing resources.

For developers and organizations, understanding the dynamics between the Resource Owner and the Relying Party is essential for building secure and user-friendly applications. Properly implementing OAuth 2.0 and OIDC flows ensures that user data is protected, while also providing a seamless experience that doesn't burden users with unnecessary complexity. Features like Single Sign-On (SSO), where users authenticate once and gain access to multiple applications, are possible because of the trust and clear roles defined between these entities.

In enterprise environments, these concepts extend beyond individual users to organizational resources. Here, the Resource Owner might be a department or a team, and the Relying Party could be an internal application accessing company data. The principles remain the same, but the stakes are higher, as mismanaging access controls can lead to data breaches or regulatory compliance issues.

Ultimately, the interplay between the Resource Owner and the Relying Party underpins the secure exchange of information in modern digital systems. By clearly defining these roles and ensuring robust mechanisms for consent, authentication, and authorization, OAuth 2.0

and OIDC provide a framework that balances security, usability, and privacy in an increasingly connected world.

OIDC Tokens: ID Token, Access Token, and Refresh Token

OpenID Connect (OIDC), built on top of OAuth 2.0, introduces a powerful identity layer that enables secure user authentication while retaining OAuth's robust authorization capabilities. Central to the operation of OIDC are three types of tokens: the ID Token, the Access Token, and the Refresh Token. Each of these tokens serves a distinct purpose in the authentication and authorization flow, ensuring that applications can securely verify user identities, access protected resources, and maintain session continuity without compromising security.

The ID Token is perhaps the most significant addition that OIDC brings to the OAuth framework. Unlike OAuth 2.0, which focuses solely on authorization, OIDC provides a standardized way to authenticate users, and the ID Token is the key to this process. The ID Token is a JSON Web Token (JWT), a compact and self-contained format that securely transmits information between parties. It contains a set of claims—pieces of information about the authenticated user and the authentication event itself. Common claims include the user's unique identifier (sub), name, email address, and the time at which the token was issued (iat).

The ID Token is digitally signed by the Identity Provider (IdP) using either symmetric or asymmetric encryption methods, ensuring its integrity and authenticity. The signature allows the Relying Party (RP), the client application that requested authentication, to verify that the token has not been tampered with and that it indeed originates from a trusted Identity Provider. This verification process is critical because it ensures that the authentication process is secure and that malicious actors cannot forge tokens to gain unauthorized access.

In addition to basic user information, the ID Token includes metadata about the authentication event, such as the issuer (iss), which identifies the Identity Provider, and the audience (aud), which specifies the intended recipient of the token, typically the client application. The token also contains an expiration time (exp), after which it is no longer valid. This time-bound nature of the ID Token ensures that authentication sessions are short-lived, reducing the risk of token misuse if intercepted.

While the ID Token is used to authenticate the user and convey identity information, the Access Token serves a different, yet equally critical, purpose. The Access Token is the means by which a client application gains access to protected resources on behalf of the user. These resources could be anything from user profile data stored on a server to APIs that the application needs to interact with. Unlike the ID Token, which is intended solely for the client's use, the Access Token is presented to resource servers to authorize specific actions or data requests.

The format of the Access Token can vary. While OIDC commonly uses JWTs for ID Tokens, Access Tokens may be in JWT format or in opaque strings that carry no readable information without validation. Regardless of format, the Access Token includes information about the scope of access granted, detailing what resources the token holder can access and what operations they are permitted to perform. For instance, an Access Token might grant read-only access to a user's contacts or full access to modify calendar events.

Access Tokens are typically short-lived, with expiration times set to minimize the security risks associated with token theft or misuse. Once an Access Token expires, the client can no longer use it to access resources unless it obtains a new one. This leads to the third key token in the OIDC framework: the Refresh Token.

The Refresh Token plays a crucial role in maintaining seamless user experiences by allowing client applications to obtain new Access Tokens without requiring the user to re-authenticate. After a user successfully authenticates and authorizes an application, the Identity Provider may issue a Refresh Token alongside the ID Token and Access Token. While the Access Token has a short lifespan, the Refresh Token is typically long-lived, enabling applications to maintain access over extended periods without disrupting the user's session.

The Refresh Token is securely stored by the client application and is never exposed to resource servers. When the Access Token expires, the client sends the Refresh Token to the Token Endpoint of the Identity Provider to request a new Access Token. The Identity Provider validates the Refresh Token and, if it's still valid, issues a new Access Token. This process allows applications to maintain continuous access while reducing the frequency of user logins, enhancing usability without compromising security.

Because Refresh Tokens provide long-term access, they are highly sensitive and must be handled with care. Best practices dictate that Refresh Tokens should be stored securely, such as in encrypted storage, and should never be exposed in client-side code, especially in public clients like single-page applications or mobile apps. Additionally, implementing token revocation mechanisms allows users and administrators to invalidate Refresh Tokens when necessary, such as in cases of account compromise or when a user logs out from all devices.

In OIDC flows, the issuance of these tokens depends on the grant type used during authentication. The most common flow, the Authorization Code Flow, is particularly secure because it involves exchanging an authorization code for tokens directly between the client and the Identity Provider's token endpoint, minimizing the risk of token interception. During this process, the client receives an ID Token, an Access Token, and optionally, a Refresh Token, depending on the application's requirements and the scopes requested.

Another security enhancement in modern OIDC implementations is the use of Proof Key for Code Exchange (PKCE). This mechanism adds an extra layer of security to the token exchange process, particularly for public clients that cannot securely store client secrets. By introducing a dynamically generated code verifier and code challenge, PKCE ensures that the authorization code cannot be intercepted and reused by malicious actors.

Understanding the distinct roles of the ID Token, Access Token, and Refresh Token is essential for developers and organizations looking to implement OIDC securely and effectively. Each token serves a specific purpose in the authentication and authorization process, working together to provide a robust, flexible, and secure framework for managing user identities and resource access. By leveraging these tokens correctly, applications can enhance user experiences, protect sensitive data, and maintain the integrity of their authentication systems in an increasingly complex digital landscape.

Authentication Flows in OIDC

OpenID Connect (OIDC) extends the OAuth 2.0 protocol by introducing an identity layer, enabling client applications to verify the identity of users and obtain basic profile information in a secure, standardized way. To accommodate a variety of application types and security requirements, OIDC defines several authentication flows. These flows outline how authentication requests and responses are handled between the client, the user, and the identity provider. Understanding these flows is essential for implementing OIDC effectively and securely in different environments.

The most commonly used flow in OIDC is the Authorization Code Flow. This flow is designed for applications that can securely store client secrets, such as server-side web applications. It operates by first redirecting the user to the identity provider's authorization endpoint, where the user authenticates and consents to share information with the client. After successful authentication, the identity provider redirects the user back to the client with an authorization code. The client then exchanges this code at the token endpoint for an ID token and, optionally, an access token and refresh token. This two-step process enhances security by ensuring that tokens are transmitted directly between the client and the identity provider over secure channels, minimizing the risk of interception.

To further secure the Authorization Code Flow, especially in public clients like mobile and single-page applications, OIDC supports Proof Key for Code Exchange (PKCE). PKCE adds an additional verification step by requiring the client to generate a code verifier and a code challenge before initiating the flow. The code challenge is sent with the authorization request, and the code verifier is used during the token exchange to confirm the client's identity. This mechanism prevents attackers from intercepting the authorization code and using it to obtain tokens, providing an extra layer of protection for less secure environments.

Another flow defined by OIDC is the Implicit Flow, which was originally intended for applications that run entirely in the user's browser, such as single-page applications (SPAs). In the Implicit Flow, tokens are issued directly from the authorization endpoint without an intermediate authorization code exchange. This approach reduces the number of network requests, making it faster but less secure because tokens are exposed in the URL and are more susceptible to interception and misuse. Due to these security concerns, the Implicit Flow is now considered less favorable, and the Authorization Code Flow with PKCE is recommended for SPAs instead.

For scenarios where applications need both the immediate issuance of tokens and the ability to obtain additional tokens later, OIDC provides the Hybrid Flow. This flow combines elements of both the Authorization Code Flow and the Implicit Flow. It allows tokens to be delivered both through the authorization response and the token endpoint. For example, an ID token might be returned immediately after authentication, while an authorization code is also provided for later exchange. This flexibility makes the Hybrid Flow suitable for applications that require a balance between immediate access and enhanced security.

OIDC also defines the Client Credentials Flow and the Resource Owner Password Credentials Flow, though these are less common in typical OIDC use cases. The Client Credentials Flow is used when an application needs to authenticate itself rather than a user, suitable for machine-to-machine communications. The Resource Owner Password Credentials Flow, where the user provides their credentials directly to the client, is generally discouraged due to security risks and is only used in highly trusted environments.

Each of these authentication flows serves specific purposes and offers varying levels of security and user experience. Selecting the appropriate flow depends on factors such as the type of application, the sensitivity of the data being accessed, and the environment in which the application operates. By understanding and correctly implementing these flows, developers can ensure secure, efficient authentication processes that protect user data and maintain the integrity of their applications.

The JSON Web Token (JWT) Format

JSON Web Tokens (JWTs) have become a cornerstone of modern authentication and authorization protocols, particularly in frameworks like OAuth 2.0 and OpenID Connect (OIDC). Designed for securely transmitting information between parties, JWTs are compact, self-contained, and versatile, making them ideal for use in distributed systems, APIs, and web applications. Understanding the JWT format and its components is essential for implementing secure and efficient authentication mechanisms.

A JWT is a string of text that represents a set of claims encoded in a standardized, secure format. It consists of three parts: the header, the payload, and the signature. These parts are separated by periods (.), creating a structure that looks like this: xxxxx.yyyyy.zzzzz. Each section serves a specific purpose, and together they ensure the integrity, authenticity, and confidentiality of the transmitted information.

The first part of the JWT is the header. The header typically consists of two fields: the type of token, which is JWT, and the signing algorithm used to secure the token, such as HMAC SHA256 (HS256) or RSA (RS256). The header is a JSON object that looks like this:

```
{

  "alg": "HS256",

  "typ": "JWT"

}
```

This JSON object is then Base64Url-encoded to create the first part of the JWT. The use of Base64Url encoding, as opposed to standard Base64, ensures that the token can be safely transmitted in URLs without issues related to special characters.

The second part of the JWT is the payload, which contains the claims. Claims are statements about an entity (typically the user) and additional metadata. There are three types of claims: registered, public, and private. Registered claims are predefined and standardized, providing essential information such as the issuer (iss), subject (sub), audience (aud), expiration time (exp), issued-at time (iat), and not-before time (nbf). These claims help manage token validity and usage context.

For example, a payload might look like this:

```
{

  "sub": "1234567890",

  "name": "John Doe",

  "admin": true,

  "iat": 1516239022

}
```

Public claims are defined by those using the JWTs and must be registered in the IANA JSON Web Token Claims registry or be defined in a way that prevents collisions. Private claims are custom claims created to share information between parties that agree on using them, such as user roles, permissions, or specific application-related data.

The payload is also Base64Url-encoded to form the second part of the JWT. It's important to note that while the payload is encoded, it is not encrypted by default, meaning the data is visible to anyone who decodes the token. For sensitive information, additional encryption should be applied, or the data should be omitted from the payload entirely.

The third part of the JWT is the signature. The signature is generated by taking the encoded header and payload, concatenating them with a period, and then signing the result using the specified algorithm and a secret key or private key. For example, if using the HMAC SHA256 algorithm, the process would be as follows:

HMACSHA256(

base64UrlEncode(header) + "." + base64UrlEncode(payload),

secret)

The resulting signature is Base64Url-encoded to create the third part of the JWT. The signature is crucial for verifying the authenticity and integrity of the token. When a JWT is received, the recipient can use the header information to determine the algorithm, then use the shared secret or public key to verify that the signature matches the header and payload. If the signature is valid, the token can be trusted as having come from the specified issuer and not having been tampered with.

JWTs are commonly used in two main scenarios: authentication and information exchange. In authentication, once the user logs in, the server generates a JWT and sends it back to the client. The client stores this token (usually in localStorage or sessionStorage in web applications) and includes it in the Authorization header of subsequent requests, typically using the Bearer schema (Authorization: Bearer <token>). The server then validates the token on each request, allowing the user to access protected resources without re-entering credentials.

In information exchange, JWTs provide a secure way to transmit claims between parties. Because JWTs are signed, the recipient can verify the data's integrity and authenticity. This makes JWTs ideal for scenarios where data must be shared securely between different components of a system, such as between microservices or across organizational boundaries.

One of the key advantages of JWTs is their statelessness. Because the token contains all the information needed for authentication and authorization, the server does not need to maintain session state or store tokens in a database. This makes JWTs highly scalable and suitable for distributed systems and microservices architectures, where maintaining centralized session state would be cumbersome.

However, the stateless nature of JWTs also introduces certain challenges. Since tokens are self-contained and typically have a fixed expiration time, revoking a token before it expires can be difficult. To address this, some systems implement token blacklisting or use short-lived tokens in combination with refresh tokens. Another concern is the potential exposure of sensitive data if not properly handled, as the payload is only encoded, not encrypted.

Security best practices are essential when implementing JWTs. Always use strong, secure algorithms for signing tokens, such as RS256, which uses a public/private key pair, rather than relying on symmetric algorithms like HS256, which require sharing a secret key. Implement proper validation checks for claims, including verifying the issuer, audience, expiration time, and other critical fields. Additionally, consider using HTTPS to protect tokens in transit and avoid exposing tokens in URLs, where they might be logged or intercepted.

In the context of OpenID Connect, JWTs are used extensively for ID Tokens, which authenticate users and provide identity information to client applications. The standardized claims in ID Tokens allow for consistent handling of user identities across different applications and platforms. OIDC's reliance on JWTs underscores their importance in modern identity and access management frameworks, highlighting their role in providing secure, efficient, and scalable authentication solutions.

The Implicit Flow

The Implicit Flow is one of the authentication methods defined in the OpenID Connect (OIDC) protocol, which itself is an identity layer built on top of OAuth 2.0. Designed primarily for public clients such as single-page applications (SPAs) and mobile apps, the Implicit Flow facilitates quick user authentication by delivering tokens directly from the authorization endpoint, without requiring an intermediate authorization code exchange. While this flow simplifies implementation and speeds up authentication, it also introduces certain security vulnerabilities, leading to a decline in its usage in favor of more secure methods like the Authorization Code Flow with Proof Key for Code Exchange (PKCE).

The Implicit Flow was initially introduced to address the needs of applications that run entirely in a user's browser or on devices that cannot securely store client secrets. Unlike traditional server-side applications, these public clients do not have a secure backend where sensitive data, such as client secrets or refresh tokens, can be safely stored. The Implicit Flow caters to this constraint by eliminating the need for such secure storage, allowing the client to receive tokens directly through the user's browser.

In the Implicit Flow, the authentication process begins when the client application redirects the user to the authorization endpoint of the identity provider. The request includes parameters specifying the desired response type, typically id_token, token, or both. The id_token is used for authenticating the user, while the token refers to the access token, which grants the application access to protected resources. Upon successful authentication, the identity provider redirects the user back to the client application, appending the tokens directly in the URL fragment.

This direct delivery of tokens streamlines the authentication process by reducing the number of network requests. Unlike the Authorization Code Flow, which involves exchanging an authorization code for tokens at the token endpoint, the Implicit Flow delivers the tokens immediately after user authentication. This makes the Implicit Flow faster and simpler to implement, particularly for applications that require quick, client-side authentication without the overhead of server-side processing.

However, the very features that make the Implicit Flow convenient also contribute to its security challenges. Since tokens are transmitted through the URL fragment, they are exposed to the browser's environment, making them vulnerable to interception by malicious scripts, browser extensions, or through accidental leakage in browser history or logs. Additionally, the absence of a backend server to securely manage the tokens means that refresh tokens are not issued in the Implicit Flow, requiring users to re-authenticate more frequently to maintain their sessions.

Another security concern arises from the lack of client authentication in the Implicit Flow. Since public clients cannot securely store client secrets, there is no mechanism to verify the authenticity of the client application making the request. This increases the risk of token theft through man-in-the-middle attacks, where attackers intercept tokens during transmission and use them to gain unauthorized access to user data.

To mitigate some of these risks, the OIDC specification recommends the use of secure communication channels, such as HTTPS, to encrypt data in transit. Additionally, developers are encouraged to implement measures like token expiration, short-lived tokens, and nonce parameters to protect against replay attacks. The nonce parameter, included in the authentication request and validated in the ID token response, ensures that the token was issued in response to a legitimate request and has not been reused or tampered with.

Despite these security measures, the Implicit Flow has fallen out of favor in recent years, particularly as the security landscape has evolved and new threats have emerged. The Authorization Code Flow with PKCE has become the recommended approach for public clients, offering a more secure alternative while maintaining the simplicity and speed required for client-side applications. PKCE adds an extra layer of verification during the authorization code exchange, effectively mitigating the risk of authorization code interception and providing stronger protection against attacks.

While the Implicit Flow may still be used in certain legacy applications or specific scenarios where quick, client-side authentication is prioritized over security, it is generally advisable to adopt more secure flows wherever possible. The shift away from the Implicit Flow reflects the broader trend towards stronger security practices in identity and access management, emphasizing the importance of safeguarding user data in an increasingly interconnected digital environment.

In summary, the Implicit Flow was developed to meet the needs of public clients that require fast, client-side authentication without secure backend storage. While it offers simplicity and speed, it also introduces significant security vulnerabilities due to the exposure of tokens in the browser environment and the lack of client authentication. As a result, the Implicit Flow is now considered less secure, with the Authorization Code Flow with PKCE emerging as the preferred method for secure authentication in modern applications. Understanding the strengths and limitations of the Implicit Flow is essential for making informed decisions about authentication strategies and ensuring the protection of user data in today's digital landscape.

The Authorization Code Flow

The Authorization Code Flow is one of the most widely used and secure authentication methods within the OpenID Connect (OIDC) and OAuth 2.0 frameworks. This flow is specifically designed for applications that can securely handle client secrets, such as server-side web applications. Its structure emphasizes security and flexibility, making it a preferred choice for developers implementing authentication in modern applications.

At its core, the Authorization Code Flow operates through a multi-step process that involves the user, the client application (also known as the Relying Party), and the Authorization Server or Identity Provider (IdP). The flow begins when the client application redirects the user to the Authorization Server's authorization endpoint. This redirection initiates the authentication process, prompting the user to log in and grant consent for the application to access specific resources on their behalf.

Once the user successfully authenticates and provides consent, the Authorization Server redirects the user back to the client application with an authorization code. This code is a temporary credential that serves as proof of the successful authentication but cannot be used directly to access resources. Instead, the client application exchanges the authorization code for tokens by making a secure request to the Authorization Server's token endpoint. During this exchange, the client must authenticate itself using its client credentials, typically a client ID and secret. This step adds an additional layer of security, ensuring that only authorized applications can complete the flow.

The tokens returned by the Authorization Server include the ID Token, the Access Token, and, optionally, a Refresh Token. The ID Token, formatted as a JSON Web Token (JWT), contains information about the authenticated user, such as their unique identifier, name, and email address. The Access Token allows the client application to access protected resources on behalf of the user, while the Refresh Token can be used to obtain new tokens without requiring the user to re-authenticate.

One of the key advantages of the Authorization Code Flow is its security. Because the tokens are exchanged on the server-side, they are never exposed to the user's browser or other potentially insecure environments. This minimizes the risk of token interception and misuse. Furthermore, the flow supports additional security mechanisms, such as Proof Key for Code Exchange (PKCE), which adds an extra layer of protection for public clients like mobile and single-page applications that cannot securely store client secrets.

PKCE enhances the Authorization Code Flow by introducing a dynamically generated code verifier and code challenge. When the client application initiates the authorization request, it generates a random code verifier and derives a code challenge from it. The code challenge is sent to the Authorization Server as part of the initial request, while the code verifier is securely stored on the client. During the token exchange, the client sends the code verifier to the Authorization Server, which verifies it against the original code challenge. This process ensures that the authorization code cannot be intercepted and reused by malicious actors.

The Authorization Code Flow also supports granular permission control through the use of scopes. Scopes define the level of access the client application is requesting from the user. For example, a calendar application might request access to read and write calendar events, while a photo-sharing app might request permission to view and upload photos. During the consent step, the user can review the requested scopes and decide whether to grant or deny access. This transparency enhances user trust and gives individuals control over their data.

In addition to its security features, the Authorization Code Flow is highly flexible and can be adapted to a variety of use cases. It is suitable for traditional web applications, as well as modern architectures that involve microservices, APIs, and federated identity systems. By leveraging the capabilities of the Authorization Code Flow, developers can implement robust authentication solutions that provide seamless user experiences while maintaining the highest standards of security.

The flow's reliance on standard protocols and tokens also ensures interoperability across different platforms and services. Applications can integrate with multiple Identity Providers, such as Google, Microsoft, and Okta, using a consistent approach. This interoperability simplifies development and maintenance, as developers can rely on well-documented standards and best practices.

Despite its strengths, implementing the Authorization Code Flow requires careful attention to detail. Developers must ensure that all endpoints are secured with HTTPS to protect sensitive data in transit. Proper validation of tokens, including verifying signatures and checking expiration times, is essential to prevent unauthorized access. Additionally, securely storing client credentials and tokens on the server is critical to maintaining the integrity of the authentication process.

The Authorization Code Flow is not limited to user authentication; it also plays a vital role in enabling Single Sign-On (SSO) across multiple applications. By leveraging a common Identity Provider, users can authenticate once and gain access to a range of services without needing to log in repeatedly. This capability enhances user convenience and reduces the administrative burden of managing multiple sets of credentials.

As the digital landscape continues to evolve, the Authorization Code Flow remains a cornerstone of secure authentication practices. Its combination of security, flexibility, and interoperability makes it an essential tool for developers and organizations looking to implement robust identity and access management solutions. By understanding and correctly applying the principles of the Authorization Code Flow, developers can build applications that protect user data, maintain trust, and provide seamless, secure experiences in an increasingly connected world.

The Hybrid Flow

The Hybrid Flow is a versatile authentication method in the OpenID Connect (OIDC) protocol, combining elements of both the Authorization Code Flow and the Implicit Flow. Designed to provide flexibility and enhanced security, the Hybrid Flow allows applications to receive tokens directly from the authorization endpoint while also obtaining additional tokens through a secure back-channel. This dual approach makes the Hybrid Flow suitable for a wide range of application types, including single-page applications (SPAs), mobile apps, and traditional web applications.

At the heart of the Hybrid Flow is its ability to return multiple tokens in a single authentication response. When a user initiates the login process, the client application redirects them to the authorization server's authorization endpoint. Unlike the Authorization Code Flow, which only returns an authorization code, or the Implicit Flow, which returns tokens directly, the Hybrid Flow can return both. This means that the client may receive an ID token and an authorization code simultaneously, or even an access token, depending on the specified response type.

The flexibility of the Hybrid Flow is evident in its support for multiple response types, such as code id_token, code token, or code id_token token. The code represents the authorization code, the id_token contains user identity information, and the token refers to the access token. By allowing combinations of these tokens, the Hybrid Flow enables applications to balance immediate access with enhanced security. For instance, an application might use the ID token for quick user authentication on the client-side while using the authorization code to securely obtain an access token from the token endpoint.

Security is a critical advantage of the Hybrid Flow. While it provides the convenience of direct token delivery, it also leverages the secure exchange of the authorization code to protect sensitive tokens. The authorization code is exchanged at the token endpoint, which typically requires client authentication using a client secret. This ensures that even if an attacker intercepts the authorization code, they cannot use it without the appropriate credentials. Additionally, the use of Proof Key for Code Exchange (PKCE) further strengthens the Hybrid Flow, particularly for public clients that cannot securely store secrets.

The Hybrid Flow also enhances user experience by reducing latency and improving responsiveness. By receiving the ID token directly from the authorization endpoint, the client can authenticate the user immediately, allowing for faster rendering of personalized content.

Meanwhile, the secure exchange of the authorization code ensures that access tokens are obtained without exposing them to potential interception in the browser environment. This balance of speed and security makes the Hybrid Flow an attractive option for applications that require both.

Another important aspect of the Hybrid Flow is its role in enabling Single Sign-On (SSO) across multiple applications. By leveraging a common identity provider and sharing authentication tokens, users can log in once and access various services without repeated authentication prompts. This seamless experience enhances user satisfaction and reduces the burden of managing multiple credentials. The Hybrid Flow's ability to provide immediate authentication tokens while maintaining secure access control supports the robust SSO capabilities of OIDC.

From a development perspective, implementing the Hybrid Flow requires careful configuration of the authorization request parameters. The client application must specify the desired response types, redirect URIs, and scopes. Scopes define the level of access requested, such as openid for basic authentication, profile for user profile information, and email for email addresses. The use of the nonce parameter is essential to prevent replay attacks, ensuring that the ID token is tied to the specific authentication request.

The Hybrid Flow also benefits from OIDC's discovery and dynamic client registration features. Through discovery, the client can automatically obtain configuration information about the identity provider, including supported response types, endpoints, and public keys for token verification. Dynamic client registration allows applications to register with the identity provider programmatically, streamlining the setup process and reducing manual configuration.

While the Hybrid Flow offers many advantages, it also requires diligent security practices. Developers must ensure that tokens are transmitted over secure channels (HTTPS), validate tokens upon receipt, and implement proper session management. Token expiration and revocation mechanisms are critical for maintaining security, particularly in scenarios where tokens are exposed in the client environment. By adhering to best practices, applications can leverage the Hybrid Flow's flexibility and security to deliver robust authentication solutions.

In summary, the Hybrid Flow represents a powerful and adaptable authentication method within the OIDC framework. By combining the strengths of the Authorization Code Flow and the Implicit Flow, it offers a balanced approach that meets the diverse needs of modern applications. Its ability to provide immediate user authentication while securing access tokens through server-side exchanges makes it a valuable tool for developers aiming to create secure, user-friendly experiences in today's digital landscape.

The Client Credentials Flow and OIDC

The Client Credentials Flow is one of the core grant types defined by OAuth 2.0 and is utilized within OpenID Connect (OIDC) when applications need to authenticate themselves rather than end-users. Unlike other flows in OIDC, which are focused on authenticating users and granting them access to resources, the Client Credentials Flow is designed for machine-to-machine (M2M) communication. In this flow, the application, acting as the client, directly requests an access token from the authorization server using its own credentials, without any involvement from a user.

The primary use case for the Client Credentials Flow is when an application needs to access its own resources or perform tasks on behalf of itself, not a specific user. For example, a background service that periodically syncs data between two systems, or a monitoring application that retrieves metrics from an API, would use this flow. Since no user is involved, the flow does not issue an ID Token, which is a critical component in other OIDC flows that deal with user authentication. Instead, the focus is entirely on issuing an Access Token that grants the application permission to interact with protected resources.

To initiate the Client Credentials Flow, the application first registers with the authorization server and obtains a client ID and client secret. These credentials uniquely identify the application and are used to authenticate it when requesting tokens. When the application needs to access a resource, it sends a token request to the authorization server's token endpoint. This request includes the client ID, client secret, and the grant_type parameter set to client_credentials. Optionally, the request can include scopes to specify the level of access the application requires.

Upon receiving the request, the authorization server verifies the client's credentials. If the credentials are valid and the application is authorized to request the specified scopes, the server issues an Access Token. This token is then used by the application to authenticate API requests to resource servers. The resource server validates the Access Token to ensure it was issued by a trusted authorization server and that it has not expired or been tampered with.

The Client Credentials Flow offers several advantages, particularly in scenarios where user interaction is not feasible or necessary. Since the flow bypasses user authentication, it simplifies the process for backend services and automated tasks. Additionally, the use of strong client authentication mechanisms, such as client secrets or mutual TLS, enhances the security of token requests. The flow also supports fine-grained access control through the use of scopes, allowing applications to request only the permissions they need.

However, the Client Credentials Flow also has its limitations. Because it does not involve user authentication, it cannot be used to access user-specific data or perform actions on behalf of a user. This makes it unsuitable for applications that require user consent or personalized services. Furthermore, the security of the flow relies heavily on the protection of client credentials. If the client secret is compromised, an attacker could potentially gain unauthorized access to protected resources. To mitigate this risk, it is essential to follow best practices for credential storage and management, such as using secure storage mechanisms and rotating secrets regularly.

In the context of OIDC, the Client Credentials Flow is somewhat of an outlier because OIDC is primarily focused on user authentication and identity management. While the flow can be used in OIDC implementations to secure machine-to-machine communications, it does not leverage the identity features that OIDC provides, such as ID Tokens and user claims. Nevertheless, it remains a valuable tool within the broader OAuth 2.0 and OIDC ecosystem, particularly for securing API interactions and automating backend processes.

Organizations that implement the Client Credentials Flow should consider integrating additional security measures, such as logging and monitoring token usage, to detect and respond to potential threats. They should also establish clear policies for managing client credentials and defining scopes to ensure that applications have the appropriate level of access. By carefully designing and managing the Client Credentials Flow, organizations can achieve secure, efficient machine-to-machine communication within their OIDC implementations.

The Password Grant Flow in Context

The Password Grant Flow, also known as the Resource Owner Password Credentials (ROPC) flow, is one of the more straightforward authentication methods defined within the OAuth 2.0 framework. Unlike other flows that use tokens, redirects, or intermediate authorization codes, the Password Grant Flow allows an application to directly collect the user's credentials (username and password) and exchange them for access tokens. While this flow may appear simple and efficient, especially in trusted environments, it comes with significant security implications that have limited its widespread adoption, particularly in modern security-conscious applications.

At its core, the Password Grant Flow works by having the client application collect the user's credentials and send them directly to the authorization server's token endpoint. This request typically includes the client ID, client secret, username, password, and the scope of access requested. Upon validating the credentials, the authorization server issues an access token, which the client application can then use to access protected resources on behalf of the user. Depending on the configuration, the authorization server may also issue a refresh token, allowing the client to obtain new access tokens without prompting the user to re-enter their credentials.

The simplicity of this flow makes it appealing for certain scenarios. For example, in first-party applications, where the client and the authorization server are both controlled by the same entity, the

Password Grant Flow can offer a seamless user experience. Users can enter their credentials directly into the application without being redirected to an external authentication page, streamlining the login process. This approach is particularly useful in applications where user experience is paramount, and the risk of credential exposure is minimal due to the trusted nature of the client.

However, the same characteristics that make the Password Grant Flow convenient also introduce significant security risks. By directly handling user credentials, the client application assumes a great deal of responsibility for securely storing and transmitting sensitive information. Any vulnerability in the client application, such as insecure storage, logging, or transmission of credentials, can expose users to the risk of credential theft and unauthorized access. This risk is exacerbated in third-party applications or public clients, where the trust between the user and the application is not guaranteed.

One of the fundamental principles of OAuth 2.0 is the separation of resource owners and clients, ensuring that applications do not need to handle user credentials directly. This principle is designed to minimize the attack surface and reduce the likelihood of credential compromise. The Password Grant Flow bypasses this safeguard, placing the burden of secure credential handling on the client application. For this reason, the flow is generally discouraged in favor of more secure alternatives, such as the Authorization Code Flow with Proof Key for Code Exchange (PKCE), which keeps credentials out of the client's hands and leverages secure token exchanges.

Despite these security concerns, the Password Grant Flow can still be useful in specific contexts. In tightly controlled environments, such as enterprise applications where the client is a trusted first-party application and the security of the communication channel is guaranteed, the flow can offer a balance of simplicity and functionality. Additionally, in legacy systems where more modern authentication methods are not feasible, the Password Grant Flow may serve as a temporary solution until more secure mechanisms can be implemented.

To mitigate the risks associated with the Password Grant Flow, several best practices should be followed. First and foremost, the client application must use secure communication protocols, such as HTTPS, to encrypt credentials in transit and protect against eavesdropping and man-in-the-middle attacks. Credentials should never be stored on the client, and sensitive information should not be logged or exposed in any way. Furthermore, multi-factor authentication (MFA) can be implemented to add an additional layer of security, ensuring that even if credentials are compromised, unauthorized access is still prevented.

Another important consideration is limiting the use of the Password Grant Flow to trusted clients and internal applications. Public clients, such as mobile or single-page applications, should avoid this flow due to the inherent risks of exposing credentials in environments where security cannot be guaranteed. In cases where public clients are involved, more secure flows like the Authorization Code Flow with PKCE should be used to ensure that credentials remain protected.

In the context of OpenID Connect, which extends OAuth 2.0 to include authentication, the Password Grant Flow can be used to obtain ID tokens in addition to access tokens. However, this approach is rarely recommended due to the same security concerns that apply to OAuth 2.0. OpenID Connect's strength lies in its ability to authenticate users without exposing their credentials to the client application, and using the Password Grant Flow undermines this advantage.

As the security landscape continues to evolve, the use of the Password Grant Flow has declined in favor of more secure and user-friendly authentication methods. Modern applications increasingly rely on federated identity systems, single sign-on (SSO) solutions, and token-based authentication flows that prioritize user privacy and security. The Password Grant Flow remains a part of the OAuth 2.0 specification, but its use is now largely confined to specific, controlled scenarios where its simplicity outweighs the potential security risks.

In summary, the Password Grant Flow offers a simple and direct method for authenticating users and obtaining access tokens. While it may be suitable for certain trusted environments, its inherent security risks make it less favorable compared to other OAuth 2.0 and OpenID Connect flows. By understanding the context in which the Password Grant Flow operates and implementing appropriate security measures, developers can make informed decisions about its use, balancing convenience with the need to protect user credentials and maintain the integrity of their applications.

Client Registration and Configuration

Client registration and configuration are foundational components in the implementation of OAuth 2.0 and OpenID Connect (OIDC). These processes establish trust between the client application and the authorization server or identity provider, enabling secure communication and access control. Proper registration and configuration ensure that client applications can authenticate users, request access tokens, and interact with protected resources in a secure and standardized manner.

The process of client registration begins when a developer or application owner registers their application with an identity provider or authorization server. This registration step is essential because it allows the identity provider to recognize the client, enforce security policies, and issue credentials that the client will use to authenticate itself during token requests. Typically, the information required during registration includes the client's name, description, and a set of redirect URIs. Redirect URIs specify where the authorization server should send responses after the user has authenticated, ensuring that tokens and authorization codes are delivered to trusted endpoints.

Once the client is registered, the authorization server issues a set of credentials, usually consisting of a client ID and a client secret. The client ID is a public identifier for the application, while the client secret is a confidential value used to authenticate the client to the authorization server. In scenarios where the client cannot securely store the secret, such as in mobile apps or single-page applications, the use of a client secret may be omitted, and additional security measures like Proof Key for Code Exchange (PKCE) are employed instead.

Configuration of the client application involves setting up the parameters and security settings required to interact with the authorization server. This includes specifying the authorization and token endpoints, defining the scopes of access, and configuring the authentication flow that the application will use. The choice of authentication flow—whether it's the Authorization Code Flow,

Implicit Flow, Hybrid Flow, or Client Credentials Flow—depends on the nature of the application and its security requirements. For example, server-side applications typically use the Authorization Code Flow with client secrets, while mobile and browser-based applications use the Authorization Code Flow with PKCE for enhanced security.

Scopes play a critical role in client configuration, as they define the level of access the client is requesting. Common scopes include openid for basic user authentication, profile for access to user profile information, and email for retrieving the user's email address. The scopes requested by the client must align with the permissions granted by the user during the authentication process. Properly configuring scopes ensures that the client only accesses the data necessary for its functionality, adhering to the principle of least privilege.

Another important aspect of client configuration is the handling of tokens. The client must be set up to securely store and manage access tokens, refresh tokens, and ID tokens. Access tokens are typically short-lived and used to authenticate API requests, while refresh tokens are used to obtain new access tokens without requiring the user to re-authenticate. ID tokens contain information about the authenticated user and are used to verify the user's identity. Ensuring that these tokens are handled securely, such as by storing them in encrypted storage and using secure communication channels, is essential for maintaining the integrity and confidentiality of the authentication process.

Dynamic client registration is a feature supported by OIDC that allows applications to register with an authorization server programmatically. This is particularly useful in environments where applications are created and deployed frequently, as it automates the registration process and reduces manual configuration. When using dynamic registration, the client sends a registration request to the authorization server's registration endpoint, including the necessary information such as redirect URIs and desired scopes. The authorization server then responds with the client credentials and configuration details needed for the application to authenticate and request tokens.

The discovery mechanism in OIDC further simplifies client configuration by providing a standardized way for clients to retrieve information about the authorization server. By accessing a well-known URL, typically formatted as https://<issuer>/.well-known/openid-configuration, the client can obtain metadata about the authorization server, including supported authentication flows, endpoints, and public keys for verifying token signatures. This dynamic discovery capability allows clients to adapt to different identity providers without hardcoding configuration details, enhancing interoperability and flexibility.

Security considerations are paramount in client registration and configuration. Developers must ensure that redirect URIs are precise and strictly defined to prevent open redirect vulnerabilities. Using wildcard characters or overly broad URIs can expose the application to attacks where tokens are redirected to malicious endpoints. Additionally, clients should use secure protocols like HTTPS for all communications with the authorization server to protect against man-in-the-middle attacks and data interception.

Proper management of client credentials is also critical. Client secrets should be stored securely and never exposed in client-side code, logs, or version control systems. In scenarios where secrets are compromised, immediate rotation and revocation mechanisms should be in place to mitigate potential risks. Regular audits of client configurations and credentials can help identify and address security vulnerabilities proactively.

In multi-tenant environments or applications that integrate with multiple identity providers, managing client registrations across different providers can become complex. Utilizing federated identity management solutions and centralized configuration management tools can streamline this process, allowing organizations to maintain consistent security policies and simplify the integration of new applications and services.

Ultimately, client registration and configuration form the backbone of secure and efficient authentication and authorization processes in OAuth 2.0 and OpenID Connect. By following best practices and leveraging the features provided by OIDC, developers can build applications that are not only secure but also scalable and adaptable to a wide range of use cases and environments. Proper registration and meticulous configuration ensure that applications interact with identity providers in a trustworthy manner, safeguarding user data and maintaining the integrity of digital interactions.

The Discovery Endpoint and Metadata

In the realm of OpenID Connect (OIDC), the Discovery Endpoint and its associated metadata play a pivotal role in simplifying client configuration and enhancing interoperability between identity providers and relying parties. The Discovery Endpoint provides a standardized way for applications to obtain necessary information about the identity provider's configuration, reducing the need for manual setup and minimizing the potential for errors. By automating the retrieval of metadata, OIDC ensures that client applications can dynamically adjust to different providers, supporting seamless integration and secure authentication processes.

The Discovery Endpoint is typically accessed via a well-known URL, following the format https://<issuer>/.well-known/openid-configuration. This URL returns a JSON document containing metadata about the identity provider, including critical information such as the authorization endpoint, token endpoint, userinfo endpoint, and supported authentication methods. This metadata serves as a blueprint for client applications, guiding them through the authentication process and ensuring they adhere to the provider's specific protocols and security requirements.

One of the key benefits of the Discovery Endpoint is its ability to provide real-time, up-to-date configuration details. Identity providers may update their endpoints, supported scopes, or cryptographic keys over time, and manually updating client configurations for each change can be cumbersome and error-prone. With the Discovery Endpoint, clients automatically retrieve the latest configuration data, ensuring that they remain compatible with the provider's infrastructure without requiring manual intervention. This dynamic approach enhances the robustness and resilience of authentication systems, allowing them to adapt to changes seamlessly.

The metadata provided by the Discovery Endpoint includes a wide range of information essential for secure and efficient authentication.

Key elements typically found in the metadata include the issuer, which identifies the identity provider; the authorization_endpoint, where users are redirected to authenticate; and the token_endpoint, where clients exchange authorization codes for tokens. Additionally, the metadata specifies the userinfo_endpoint, which clients use to retrieve user profile information, and the jwks_uri, which points to the JSON Web Key Set (JWKS) used to verify the signatures of tokens issued by the provider.

Another important aspect of the metadata is the list of supported scopes and response types. Scopes define the level of access requested by the client, such as openid for basic authentication, profile for user profile information, and email for accessing the user's email address. Response types indicate the types of tokens that the provider can issue, such as code, id_token, or token. By specifying these details in the metadata, the identity provider ensures that clients request appropriate permissions and understand the expected responses, fostering secure and predictable interactions.

The Discovery Endpoint also outlines the supported grant types, which define the methods by which clients can obtain tokens. Common grant types include the Authorization Code Flow, Implicit Flow, Hybrid Flow, and Client Credentials Flow. By listing supported grant types in the metadata, the identity provider informs clients of the available authentication mechanisms, allowing them to choose the most suitable flow for their application architecture and security requirements.

Security is a central concern in the use of the Discovery Endpoint and metadata. The integrity and authenticity of the metadata must be ensured to prevent malicious actors from manipulating configuration details and compromising the authentication process. To address this, identity providers typically serve the metadata over secure HTTPS connections, protecting it from tampering and eavesdropping during transmission. Clients should also validate the issuer value in the metadata to ensure it matches the expected identity provider, safeguarding against potential impersonation attacks.

In addition to static configuration data, the Discovery Endpoint provides dynamic information about the identity provider's cryptographic keys through the jwks_uri. The JSON Web Key Set (JWKS) contains public keys used to verify the signatures of tokens issued by the provider. By retrieving the JWKS from the specified URI, clients can validate tokens without requiring prior knowledge of the provider's keys. This dynamic key management enhances security by allowing identity providers to rotate keys as needed, reducing the risk of key compromise while maintaining uninterrupted service.

The Discovery Endpoint's ability to standardize and automate configuration extends beyond individual applications to support federated identity systems and multi-tenant environments. In federated systems, multiple organizations may rely on a central identity provider for authentication, and the Discovery Endpoint ensures that all participating clients can obtain consistent configuration data. In multi-tenant scenarios, where a single application serves multiple organizations with different identity providers, the Discovery Endpoint enables dynamic adaptation to each provider's configuration, simplifying integration and maintenance.

While the Discovery Endpoint offers significant advantages in terms of automation and security, it also introduces certain challenges. Clients must handle potential failures in retrieving or parsing metadata, such as network issues or malformed JSON responses. Implementing robust error handling and fallback mechanisms is essential to ensure that authentication processes remain reliable even in the face of such issues. Additionally, clients should periodically refresh the metadata to capture any updates from the identity provider, balancing the need for up-to-date information with considerations for network efficiency.

In summary, the Discovery Endpoint and its associated metadata are integral components of the OpenID Connect protocol, facilitating dynamic configuration and secure interoperability between identity providers and client applications. By automating the retrieval of critical configuration details, the Discovery Endpoint enhances the flexibility, security, and resilience of authentication systems, supporting a wide range of applications and use cases in today's interconnected digital landscape.

Understanding Scopes and Claims

In the OpenID Connect (OIDC) protocol, scopes and claims are fundamental concepts that govern how identity and access management is handled between clients, users, and identity providers. They work together to define what information a client application can access and how much control a user has over sharing their personal data. Understanding the roles of scopes and claims is essential for implementing secure, efficient, and privacy-conscious authentication systems.

Scopes in OIDC are used to specify the level of access a client application is requesting from an identity provider. When a client initiates an authentication request, it includes one or more scopes that define what resources or information it wishes to access. The most basic and required scope in any OIDC request is openid, which signals to the identity provider that the client is requesting authentication via OpenID Connect. Without this scope, the authentication request defaults to a standard OAuth 2.0 authorization request, which does not return identity-related information.

Beyond the openid scope, additional scopes can be included to request specific pieces of user information. Common examples include profile, email, address, and phone. The profile scope requests access to standard profile information such as the user's name, preferred username, and profile picture. The email scope allows the client to access the user's email address and its verification status, while the address and phone scopes grant access to the user's physical address and phone number, respectively. Each of these scopes corresponds to a set of claims that are returned in the ID token or can be retrieved from the UserInfo endpoint after authentication.

Claims are the actual pieces of information about the user that are provided by the identity provider. They are named attributes or assertions that describe specific characteristics of the authenticated user. Claims can be included in the ID token, which is a JSON Web Token (JWT) issued during the authentication process, or they can be accessed from the UserInfo endpoint using an access token. Claims provide the data that client applications use to personalize user experiences, enforce authorization decisions, and maintain accurate records of user identity.

There are three categories of claims in OIDC: registered claims, public claims, and private claims. Registered claims are standardized and defined by the OIDC specification to ensure consistency across implementations. These include claims like sub (subject identifier), which uniquely identifies the user; iss (issuer), which identifies the identity provider; aud (audience), specifying the intended recipients of the token; exp (expiration time), indicating when the token will expire; and iat (issued at), noting when the token was issued. Registered claims also cover user-specific information like name, email, and birthdate, which are commonly used in applications that require user personalization.

Public claims are those that can be freely defined and registered with the IANA JSON Web Token Claims registry. These claims are intended for general use across different applications and identity providers but require a level of standardization to prevent naming conflicts. For instance, an organization might define a public claim to represent a user's department within a company, making it easier for applications to recognize and utilize this information consistently.

Private claims, on the other hand, are custom claims created for use between specific clients and identity providers. These claims are not standardized and are intended for use in scenarios where proprietary or unique information needs to be shared. For example, a private claim might indicate a user's membership level in a subscription service or their specific permissions within an application. Because private claims are not standardized, both the client and the identity provider must agree on their meaning and usage.

The relationship between scopes and claims is straightforward but important. When a client requests certain scopes, the identity provider responds by including the corresponding claims in the ID token or making them available through the UserInfo endpoint. However, the inclusion of these claims depends on user consent and the identity provider's policies. Users are typically prompted to approve or deny access to the requested scopes during the authentication process, allowing them to control what information is shared with the client.

This consent mechanism is a critical aspect of privacy protection in OIDC, ensuring that users have visibility and control over their personal data.

From a security perspective, scopes and claims help enforce the principle of least privilege, which dictates that applications should only request and access the minimum amount of information necessary to perform their functions. By carefully selecting the appropriate scopes and limiting the claims requested, developers can reduce the risk of overexposing sensitive user data and minimize the impact of potential security breaches. Identity providers also play a role in enforcing this principle by restricting access to certain claims based on the client's trust level or the user's preferences.

Claims in the ID token are particularly important for session management and user identification within applications. Since the ID token is issued immediately after authentication, it provides a reliable way for applications to verify the user's identity without needing to make additional network requests. This improves performance and user experience, especially in scenarios where quick authentication is essential. However, because the ID token is a self-contained JWT, it must be validated by the client to ensure its authenticity and integrity. This involves checking the token's signature, verifying the iss and aud claims, and confirming that the token has not expired.

For more dynamic or sensitive data, applications can use the access token to retrieve claims from the UserInfo endpoint. This method ensures that the information is current and allows the identity provider to apply additional security checks before releasing the data. The UserInfo endpoint is particularly useful for applications that need to display up-to-date user profile information or verify specific attributes after the initial authentication.

In federated identity scenarios, where multiple organizations or services share authentication infrastructure, scopes and claims play an even more critical role in standardizing identity information across diverse systems. By adhering to OIDC's standardized claims and scopes, federated systems can ensure consistent handling of user data, simplifying integration and enhancing interoperability. This is especially important in enterprise environments, where users may need to access a variety of applications with a single set of credentials.

In summary, scopes and claims are fundamental elements of OpenID Connect that define the information a client can request and receive from an identity provider. Scopes specify the level of access, while claims provide detailed information about the user. Together, they facilitate secure, efficient, and privacy-respecting authentication processes, supporting a wide range of applications and use cases in today's digital landscape. By understanding and implementing scopes and claims effectively, developers can build applications that respect user privacy, enforce security best practices, and deliver personalized, user-centric experiences.

Securing OIDC with PKCE

Proof Key for Code Exchange, commonly known as PKCE (pronounced "pixy"), is a security extension to the OAuth 2.0 Authorization Code Flow. It was originally designed to enhance the security of public clients such as mobile and single-page applications, which cannot securely store client secrets. In the context of OpenID Connect (OIDC), PKCE plays a critical role in securing the authentication process, protecting against various attack vectors, and ensuring the integrity of authorization requests.

The Authorization Code Flow is widely regarded as the most secure method for handling authentication and authorization in OAuth 2.0 and OIDC. It involves redirecting the user to the authorization server, where they authenticate and authorize access, and then returning an authorization code to the client application. This code is exchanged for tokens, including the ID Token and Access Token, at the token endpoint. While the flow itself is secure for confidential clients like server-side applications, it is vulnerable to interception attacks when used by public clients that cannot safeguard client secrets. This is where PKCE comes into play.

PKCE mitigates the risk of authorization code interception attacks by introducing an additional layer of verification during the authorization code exchange. The process begins when the client application generates a random string called the code verifier. This verifier is then transformed into a code challenge using a cryptographic hash function, typically SHA-256. The code challenge is included in the initial authorization request sent to the authorization server. When the user completes the authentication and authorization steps, the server returns the authorization code to the client, as usual.

The key difference with PKCE occurs during the token exchange. To redeem the authorization code for tokens, the client must send the original code verifier to the authorization server. The server then applies the same hash function to the verifier and compares the result to the code challenge received earlier. If the two match, the server knows that the client requesting the tokens is the same one that initiated the authorization request, effectively preventing any malicious actor from using an intercepted authorization code.

This additional verification step significantly enhances the security of the Authorization Code Flow, making it suitable for public clients that operate in less secure environments. Mobile applications, for example, are distributed to user devices where the code can be inspected and manipulated, making it impossible to keep client secrets secure. Similarly, single-page applications run entirely in the user's browser, exposing them to the risk of malicious scripts or browser extensions intercepting sensitive data. PKCE addresses these vulnerabilities by eliminating the need for client secrets and ensuring that authorization codes cannot be misused if intercepted.

The adoption of PKCE has become a best practice not only for public clients but also for confidential clients. Even though server-side applications can securely store client secrets, using PKCE adds an extra layer of security that protects against certain advanced attack vectors, such as authorization server misconfiguration or compromised network environments. By standardizing the use of PKCE across all client types, developers can create more secure and consistent authentication implementations.

In addition to securing the Authorization Code Flow, PKCE integrates seamlessly with other OIDC features to provide comprehensive protection. The use of the nonce parameter in OIDC helps prevent replay attacks by ensuring that ID Tokens are tied to specific authentication requests. When combined with PKCE, the nonce and code challenge mechanisms work together to secure both the authorization and authentication aspects of the flow. This dual-layer protection is especially important in scenarios where sensitive user information is being accessed or where high levels of security are required, such as in financial or healthcare applications.

Implementing PKCE in an OIDC-enabled application involves several straightforward steps. The client application must generate a high-entropy, cryptographically random code verifier. This verifier should be unique for each authorization request and stored securely until the token exchange. The code verifier is then hashed using SHA-256 to produce the code challenge, which is sent to the authorization server along with the standard authorization request parameters, such as the client ID, redirect URI, and requested scopes.

The authorization server must support PKCE and be configured to recognize and validate the code challenge and verifier. Upon receiving the token request, the server compares the code verifier to the original code challenge, ensuring that they match before issuing tokens. If the server detects any discrepancies or if the code verifier is missing, it should reject the token request, preventing unauthorized access.

One of the advantages of PKCE is that it requires minimal changes to existing OIDC implementations. Most modern identity providers and authorization servers, including those from major cloud providers like Google, Microsoft, and Autho, support PKCE out of the box. This widespread support makes it easy for developers to adopt PKCE without significant refactoring of their applications or authentication flows. Additionally, many OIDC client libraries and SDKs provide built-in support for PKCE, further simplifying the implementation process.

While PKCE enhances the security of the Authorization Code Flow, it is important to remember that it is not a standalone security solution. It should be used in conjunction with other best practices, such as using secure communication channels (HTTPS), validating tokens properly, and implementing strong session management. Developers should also be vigilant about keeping their dependencies and libraries up to date to protect against known vulnerabilities.

As the security landscape continues to evolve, PKCE represents a critical advancement in securing OAuth 2.0 and OIDC flows. Its ability to protect against authorization code interception and its seamless integration with existing authentication mechanisms make it an essential tool for developers building secure applications. By adopting PKCE, organizations can enhance the security of their authentication processes, protect user data, and ensure the integrity of their digital interactions.

The Role of the UserInfo Endpoint

In the OpenID Connect (OIDC) protocol, the UserInfo endpoint plays a pivotal role in the process of user authentication and identity management. While the ID token provides essential information about an authenticated user, the UserInfo endpoint allows client applications to retrieve additional claims about the user from the identity provider. This interaction enriches the user profile information accessible to relying parties and enhances the functionality and personalization of applications, all while adhering to standardized security and privacy protocols.

The UserInfo endpoint is an OAuth 2.0 protected resource, meaning that access to it requires a valid access token. After a user successfully authenticates via OIDC and the client application receives an ID token and access token, the application can use the access token to make a secure request to the UserInfo endpoint. The identity provider then responds with a JSON object containing various claims about the user, such as their name, email address, profile picture, and other attributes, depending on the scopes requested during authentication and the user's consent.

One of the primary benefits of the UserInfo endpoint is that it allows for a separation between authentication and detailed user information retrieval. The ID token, which is received during the initial authentication process, contains only a limited set of claims necessary to establish the user's identity and verify the authentication process. However, applications often need more detailed information to personalize user experiences or manage user-specific data. By querying the UserInfo endpoint, applications can access this additional information without overloading the ID token with unnecessary data, keeping tokens lightweight and efficient.

The flexibility of the UserInfo endpoint is evident in its support for various scopes that define the level of access and the type of information the client application can retrieve. For example, the openid scope is required for basic authentication, while additional scopes like profile, email, address, and phone grant access to specific categories of user information. This scope-based access control ensures that users have granular control over what information they share with each application, enhancing privacy and data protection.

Security is a fundamental aspect of the UserInfo endpoint. Since it is an OAuth 2.0 protected resource, the endpoint requires a valid access token for any data retrieval request. This ensures that only authorized applications that have successfully completed the authentication process can access user information. Furthermore, the identity provider is responsible for verifying the validity of the access token before responding with user data, protecting against unauthorized access and token misuse.

The response from the UserInfo endpoint is typically a JSON object containing a set of claims about the user. These claims are standardized in the OIDC specification, but they can also include custom claims defined by the identity provider or specific to the application's needs. Standard claims include sub (subject identifier), name, given_name, family_name, email, and preferred_username. The sub claim is particularly important as it provides a unique identifier for the user that remains consistent across sessions and interactions, allowing applications to reliably associate data and activities with the correct user.

One of the key advantages of using the UserInfo endpoint is the ability to maintain up-to-date user information. Since the endpoint queries the identity provider in real time, it reflects the most current data about the user. This is particularly useful in scenarios where user attributes may change frequently, such as updates to contact information, profile pictures, or user roles. By leveraging the UserInfo endpoint, applications can ensure that they always present the most accurate and current information to the user.

The UserInfo endpoint also plays a crucial role in federated identity scenarios, where users authenticate using an external identity provider. In such cases, the UserInfo endpoint allows relying parties to retrieve user attributes from the federated provider, ensuring that applications have consistent access to user data regardless of the authentication source. This capability is essential for enabling seamless Single Sign-On (SSO) experiences across different applications and domains, as it allows user information to flow securely and consistently between systems.

While the UserInfo endpoint enhances the richness of user data available to applications, it also introduces important considerations regarding privacy and data minimization. Applications should request only the scopes necessary for their functionality, and users should be clearly informed about what data will be accessed and how it will be used. Identity providers can enforce policies that limit the scope of data shared based on organizational requirements or regulatory compliance, ensuring that user privacy is respected and protected.

Implementing the UserInfo endpoint requires careful attention to secure communication and proper token management. All requests to the endpoint must be made over HTTPS to protect against eavesdropping and man-in-the-middle attacks. Access tokens should be securely stored and handled within the client application, and token expiration and revocation mechanisms should be in place to minimize the risk of unauthorized access. Additionally, applications should validate the integrity of the data received from the UserInfo endpoint, ensuring that it matches the expected claims and has not been tampered with.

In summary, the UserInfo endpoint is a critical component of the OpenID Connect protocol, enabling applications to retrieve comprehensive user information securely and efficiently. By providing a standardized mechanism for accessing user claims, the UserInfo endpoint supports enhanced personalization, seamless SSO experiences, and robust identity management across diverse application ecosystems. Through careful implementation and adherence to security best practices, the UserInfo endpoint helps ensure that user data is handled responsibly, supporting both functionality and privacy in modern digital interactions.

Using OIDC in Single Sign-On (SSO)

Single Sign-On (SSO) has become a fundamental feature in modern identity management systems, enabling users to authenticate once and gain access to multiple applications without repeatedly entering their credentials. OpenID Connect (OIDC), an identity layer built on top of the OAuth 2.0 protocol, plays a crucial role in enabling SSO by providing a standardized framework for secure and seamless authentication across diverse platforms and services. Understanding how OIDC integrates with SSO is essential for developers and organizations aiming to enhance user experience, streamline access control, and maintain robust security.

At its core, SSO with OIDC revolves around the concept of a centralized identity provider (IdP) that handles user authentication on behalf of various client applications, also known as relying parties. When a user attempts to access an application that supports OIDC-based SSO, the application redirects the user to the identity provider for authentication. The identity provider verifies the user's credentials and, upon successful authentication, issues an ID token and an access token. These tokens are then used by the client application to establish the user's identity and grant access to protected resources.

One of the key advantages of using OIDC for SSO is its ability to provide a consistent and interoperable authentication experience across different applications and platforms. OIDC relies on standard protocols and token formats, such as JSON Web Tokens (JWT), to transmit identity information securely and efficiently. This standardization ensures that applications from different vendors or development environments can integrate with the same identity provider, simplifying the implementation of SSO in complex, multi-application ecosystems.

The ID token issued by the identity provider is central to the SSO process. It contains a set of claims that describe the authenticated user, such as their unique identifier (sub), name, email address, and other profile information. The client application validates the ID token to confirm the user's identity and establish an authenticated session. Since the ID token is digitally signed by the identity provider, it provides a tamper-proof mechanism for verifying the authenticity of the user's identity, enhancing the security of the SSO process.

In addition to the ID token, the access token plays a critical role in enabling SSO across applications that need to access user-specific resources or APIs. The access token grants the client application permission to interact with resource servers on behalf of the user, facilitating seamless integration between authentication and authorization processes. This capability is particularly useful in scenarios where users need to access shared resources or services across multiple applications, such as in enterprise environments or federated identity systems.

The use of OIDC in SSO also enhances user experience by reducing the cognitive load associated with managing multiple sets of credentials. With SSO, users only need to remember one set of login credentials, which they use to authenticate with the identity provider. Once authenticated, they can access all connected applications without being prompted to log in again. This streamlined experience not only improves user satisfaction but also reduces the likelihood of password-related security issues, such as weak or reused passwords.

From an organizational perspective, implementing SSO with OIDC offers significant benefits in terms of security, compliance, and administrative efficiency. Centralizing authentication with a trusted identity provider allows organizations to enforce consistent security policies, such as multi-factor authentication (MFA), across all applications. This centralized approach also simplifies auditing and compliance reporting, as authentication logs and access records are consolidated in a single location. Additionally, managing user access and permissions becomes more straightforward, as administrators can control access rights from a central directory or identity management system.

The flexibility of OIDC-based SSO extends to various authentication flows that cater to different application architectures and security requirements. The Authorization Code Flow is the most common flow used in SSO implementations, particularly for server-side applications that can securely store client secrets. This flow involves redirecting the user to the identity provider for authentication and then exchanging an authorization code for tokens at the token endpoint. The use of Proof Key for Code Exchange (PKCE) enhances the security of this flow, especially for public clients like mobile apps and single-page applications.

For applications that require immediate access to user information without the need for a server-side token exchange, the Implicit Flow can be used, although it is generally discouraged due to security concerns. The Hybrid Flow offers a balance between the Authorization Code Flow and the Implicit Flow, allowing applications to receive tokens both directly from the authorization endpoint and through the token endpoint. By supporting multiple authentication flows, OIDC provides the flexibility needed to implement SSO in a wide range of scenarios and environments.

In federated identity scenarios, OIDC-based SSO enables users to authenticate with external identity providers while maintaining a seamless experience across applications. For example, an organization might allow employees to log in to third-party applications using their corporate credentials, leveraging an external identity provider like Google or Microsoft Azure Active Directory. This federated approach simplifies access to external services while maintaining control over authentication and security policies within the organization.

Security is a paramount consideration in any SSO implementation, and OIDC provides several mechanisms to ensure the integrity and confidentiality of the authentication process. Tokens are signed and can be encrypted to prevent tampering and unauthorized access. The use of secure communication channels, such as HTTPS, protects tokens and authentication requests from interception during transmission. Additionally, features like token expiration, revocation, and audience validation help prevent token misuse and ensure that tokens are only valid for the intended applications.

Another important aspect of OIDC-based SSO is session management. The identity provider maintains the user's authentication session, allowing users to remain logged in across multiple applications without re-entering their credentials. Session management features, such as session timeout and single logout (SLO), provide control over session duration and termination, enhancing security while maintaining user convenience. Single logout ensures that when a user logs out from one application, their session is terminated across all connected applications, reducing the risk of unauthorized access due to forgotten sessions.

OIDC's support for dynamic client registration and discovery mechanisms further simplifies the implementation of SSO. Dynamic client registration allows applications to register with the identity provider programmatically, reducing the need for manual configuration. The discovery mechanism provides a standardized way for applications to retrieve configuration information about the identity provider, such as endpoints, supported scopes, and public keys for token verification. These features enhance the scalability and maintainability of SSO implementations, particularly in large, dynamic environments.

In summary, using OIDC in Single Sign-On (SSO) offers a robust, secure, and standardized approach to managing user authentication across multiple applications. By centralizing authentication with a trusted identity provider and leveraging standard protocols and token formats, OIDC-based SSO enhances user experience, simplifies access management, and strengthens security. Its flexibility, interoperability, and support for various authentication flows make it an ideal solution for organizations seeking to streamline identity management and provide seamless, secure access to digital resources in an increasingly connected world.

Federation with OIDC

Federation in the context of identity management refers to the establishment of trust relationships between different organizations or domains, allowing users to authenticate with one system and access resources across multiple systems seamlessly. OpenID Connect (OIDC) plays a crucial role in enabling this federated identity model by providing a standardized protocol for authentication and authorization. Through OIDC, organizations can simplify user management, enhance security, and deliver a unified user experience across diverse platforms.

The core concept behind federation with OIDC is the ability for an identity provider (IdP) in one domain to authenticate users and pass that authentication information to relying parties (RPs) in other domains. This trust relationship means that users can log in once with their home organization's credentials and access services offered by other organizations without needing to create separate accounts or manage multiple sets of credentials. This is particularly useful in scenarios involving partnerships between companies, educational institutions collaborating on shared platforms, or government services that require unified access across various departments.

OIDC achieves this federated model by building on the OAuth 2.0 authorization framework, adding an identity layer that enables secure user authentication. When a user attempts to access a resource provided by a relying party, the RP redirects the user to the IdP for authentication. After the user successfully logs in, the IdP issues an ID token and, optionally, an access token. The ID token contains claims about the user's identity, such as their unique identifier, name, and email address. The RP then verifies the token's authenticity and grants the user access to the requested resources.

One of the key strengths of OIDC in federated environments is its support for standardized claims and scopes. Claims are pieces of information about the user included in the ID token, while scopes define the level of access the RP is requesting. Standardized claims ensure that identity information is consistent and interoperable across different systems, making it easier for organizations to integrate their services. For example, an RP in one organization can expect the same sub (subject identifier) or email claim format from an IdP in another organization, facilitating smooth authentication and authorization processes.

Another critical aspect of federation with OIDC is the use of discovery and dynamic client registration features. The discovery mechanism allows RPs to automatically obtain configuration information about an IdP, such as its authorization and token endpoints, supported scopes, and public keys for verifying tokens. This reduces the need for manual configuration and ensures that RPs always have up-to-date information about their federated IdPs. Dynamic client registration further simplifies the process by allowing RPs to register with IdPs programmatically, enabling scalable and flexible federation across multiple domains.

Security is a paramount concern in federated identity systems, and OIDC incorporates several mechanisms to protect against common threats. The use of JSON Web Tokens (JWTs) for ID tokens ensures that identity information is securely transmitted and can be verified for authenticity and integrity. Tokens are signed using cryptographic keys, and RPs validate these signatures to confirm that the tokens were issued by trusted IdPs. Additionally, OIDC supports Proof Key for Code Exchange (PKCE) to prevent authorization code interception attacks, particularly in public clients like mobile or single-page applications.

Federation with OIDC also addresses the need for single sign-on (SSO) capabilities across federated systems. SSO allows users to authenticate once with their home IdP and access multiple services across different organizations without needing to log in again. This seamless experience enhances user convenience and productivity while reducing the burden of managing multiple credentials. It also improves security by centralizing authentication processes and enabling organizations to enforce consistent security policies, such as multi-factor authentication (MFA) or conditional access controls.

In addition to simplifying user access, federation with OIDC provides significant administrative benefits. By delegating authentication responsibilities to a central IdP, organizations can streamline user provisioning and de-provisioning processes. When a user's status changes, such as when they join or leave an organization, these changes are reflected across all federated services automatically. This reduces the administrative overhead of managing user accounts in multiple systems and ensures that access to sensitive resources is promptly updated or revoked as needed.

Federation with OIDC is particularly valuable in multi-organizational collaborations, such as consortiums, research partnerships, or supply chain networks. In these scenarios, different entities need to share resources and data securely while maintaining control over their own identity management systems. OIDC allows each organization to act as its own IdP, while establishing trust relationships with other organizations to enable federated access. This decentralized approach preserves organizational autonomy while facilitating secure collaboration.

Despite its many advantages, implementing federation with OIDC requires careful planning and coordination between participating organizations. Establishing trust relationships involves configuring mutual agreements on token validation, claim mappings, and security policies. Organizations must also ensure that their IdPs and RPs are compliant with OIDC standards and capable of handling the necessary authentication and authorization flows. Regular audits and security assessments are essential to maintain the integrity of federated systems and address potential vulnerabilities.

Federation with OIDC also raises important considerations regarding privacy and data sharing. Organizations must be transparent with users about what identity information will be shared across federated services and obtain appropriate consent where required. Data minimization practices should be implemented to ensure that only the necessary information is exchanged, protecting user privacy while enabling secure access. Additionally, clear policies and agreements should be established between federated partners to govern data usage, retention, and security practices.

In summary, federation with OpenID Connect provides a powerful framework for enabling secure, seamless access across multiple organizations and domains. By leveraging standardized protocols, robust security mechanisms, and flexible configuration options, OIDC facilitates the creation of federated identity systems that enhance user experience, streamline administration, and support collaborative initiatives. As digital ecosystems continue to expand and organizations increasingly rely on interconnected services, federation with OIDC will play a critical role in ensuring secure and efficient identity management in a complex, multi-entity environment.

OIDC and Mobile Applications

OpenID Connect (OIDC) has become a cornerstone for secure, standardized user authentication across various digital platforms, including mobile applications. As mobile devices continue to dominate the digital landscape, ensuring secure and seamless authentication experiences on these platforms is more important than ever. OIDC provides a framework that not only enhances the security of mobile applications but also simplifies the process of managing user identities across different systems and services.

Mobile applications present unique challenges and requirements for authentication compared to traditional web applications. Unlike server-side applications that can securely store client secrets and manage session states, mobile applications are distributed to user devices where code and stored data are more vulnerable to tampering and unauthorized access. This environment necessitates the use of authentication methods that do not rely on the confidentiality of client secrets. OIDC addresses this need through the Authorization Code Flow with Proof Key for Code Exchange (PKCE), which offers a secure, robust authentication process tailored for public clients like mobile apps.

The Authorization Code Flow with PKCE is particularly suited for mobile applications because it mitigates the risks associated with authorization code interception. In a typical scenario, when a user initiates authentication, the mobile application generates a unique, high-entropy code verifier and transforms it into a code challenge using a hashing algorithm like SHA-256. This code challenge is included in the authorization request sent to the identity provider. After the user successfully authenticates, the identity provider returns an authorization code to the application. To exchange this code for tokens, the application must present the original code verifier to the identity provider, which verifies it against the initial code challenge. This process ensures that the authorization code cannot be reused by malicious actors even if intercepted.

The use of PKCE in mobile applications not only secures the exchange of tokens but also simplifies the development process. Developers do not need to manage or protect client secrets, reducing the complexity and potential vulnerabilities in the application. This makes OIDC with PKCE an ideal choice for both iOS and Android platforms, where maintaining the confidentiality of embedded secrets is inherently challenging.

Another key advantage of using OIDC in mobile applications is its support for federated identity management and Single Sign-On (SSO) capabilities. With OIDC, mobile applications can integrate with a variety of identity providers, allowing users to authenticate using their existing credentials from services like Google, Microsoft, or corporate identity systems. This reduces the need for users to remember multiple passwords and enhances the overall user experience by providing quick and consistent access across different applications and services.

Integrating OIDC into mobile applications also supports better user management and data security. Through the use of standardized scopes and claims, applications can request only the information they need, adhering to the principle of least privilege. This not only minimizes the exposure of user data but also provides transparency, as users can see exactly what information the application is requesting during the consent process. Claims returned in the ID token or accessed via the UserInfo endpoint can include essential details such as the user's name, email, and profile picture, which can be used to personalize the user experience within the app.

Security considerations are paramount when implementing OIDC in mobile applications. While PKCE addresses many of the challenges related to secure token exchange, developers must also ensure that tokens are handled securely after they are issued. This includes storing tokens in secure, encrypted storage provided by the mobile operating system, such as the iOS Keychain or Android's EncryptedSharedPreferences. Additionally, developers should implement proper token expiration and refresh mechanisms, using refresh tokens to maintain user sessions without requiring frequent re-authentication.

The user interface and experience in mobile applications also play a crucial role in the implementation of OIDC. Redirecting users to an external browser for authentication, known as using an external user-agent, is a common practice that enhances security by isolating the authentication process from the application itself. This approach prevents the application from accessing user credentials directly and leverages the security features of modern browsers. Alternatively, in-app browsers or embedded web views can be used, but they require additional security measures to ensure that user credentials are not compromised.

Error handling and user feedback are critical components of a successful OIDC integration in mobile applications. Applications should gracefully handle scenarios where authentication fails, tokens expire, or network connectivity is lost. Providing clear, user-friendly messages and recovery options helps maintain a smooth user experience and reduces frustration. Additionally, logging and monitoring authentication processes can help developers identify and address potential issues, ensuring that the application remains secure and reliable.

The adoption of OIDC in mobile applications also facilitates compliance with regulatory requirements and industry standards for data protection and privacy. By leveraging a standardized, well-documented authentication protocol, developers can ensure that their applications meet security best practices and are prepared for audits and assessments. This is particularly important in industries like healthcare, finance, and education, where protecting user data is critical.

In the evolving landscape of mobile development, OIDC continues to provide a flexible, secure foundation for user authentication and identity management. Its compatibility with modern security standards, support for federated identities, and adaptability to the unique challenges of mobile environments make it an indispensable tool for developers aiming to create secure, user-friendly mobile applications. As mobile technology continues to advance, the role of OIDC in ensuring secure, seamless authentication experiences will only become more significant, driving innovation and trust in mobile ecosystems worldwide.

OIDC in Single Page Applications (SPAs)

Single Page Applications (SPAs) have revolutionized web development by providing dynamic, fast, and responsive user experiences. Unlike traditional multi-page applications, SPAs load a single HTML page and dynamically update the content as the user interacts with the application, typically through JavaScript frameworks like React,

Angular, or Vue.js. While this architectural approach offers significant performance and usability benefits, it also introduces unique challenges in securing user authentication and managing sessions. OpenID Connect (OIDC), an identity layer built on top of OAuth 2.0, provides a robust framework for addressing these challenges, offering standardized protocols and security mechanisms tailored to the needs of SPAs.

SPAs run entirely on the client side, meaning that sensitive data and application logic are exposed in the browser environment. This exposure makes SPAs particularly vulnerable to security threats such as cross-site scripting (XSS) attacks, token theft, and unauthorized access. One of the primary concerns in SPA security is managing user authentication in a way that does not compromise the integrity of the user's credentials or tokens. OIDC addresses these concerns by leveraging the Authorization Code Flow with Proof Key for Code Exchange (PKCE), a method specifically designed to enhance security in public clients like SPAs that cannot securely store client secrets.

The Authorization Code Flow with PKCE works by introducing an additional layer of verification during the authentication process. When a user attempts to log in to an SPA, the application generates a unique code verifier and derives a code challenge from it using a cryptographic hash function such as SHA-256. The application then redirects the user to the identity provider's authorization endpoint, including the code challenge in the request. After the user authenticates, the identity provider returns an authorization code to the application. To exchange this code for tokens, the application sends the original code verifier to the identity provider, which verifies that it matches the initial code challenge before issuing the tokens. This process ensures that the authorization code cannot be intercepted and used by malicious actors, even in a vulnerable client-side environment.

The use of PKCE in SPAs not only secures the token exchange but also eliminates the need for client secrets, which cannot be safely stored in a browser. This makes the Authorization Code Flow with PKCE the recommended approach for SPAs, replacing the previously common Implicit Flow, which exposed tokens directly in the URL and posed significant security risks. The transition from the Implicit Flow to the

Authorization Code Flow with PKCE represents a shift towards more secure authentication practices in SPA development, aligning with modern security standards and best practices.

Integrating OIDC into SPAs also enhances user experience by enabling seamless Single Sign-On (SSO) capabilities and federated identity management. With OIDC, SPAs can integrate with a variety of identity providers, allowing users to authenticate using their existing credentials from providers like Google, Microsoft, or enterprise identity systems. This reduces the need for users to create and manage multiple accounts, streamlining the login process and improving user satisfaction. Additionally, OIDC's support for standardized scopes and claims allows SPAs to request and receive specific pieces of user information, such as the user's name, email address, and profile picture, which can be used to personalize the application and enhance user engagement.

Security remains a critical consideration when handling tokens in SPAs. Access tokens and ID tokens, once obtained, must be securely stored to prevent unauthorized access. Since SPAs operate in a client-side environment, developers must avoid storing tokens in insecure locations like local storage or session storage, which are susceptible to XSS attacks. Instead, tokens should be stored in memory, accessible only during the active session, and cleared when the application is closed or the user logs out. This approach minimizes the risk of token theft while maintaining session integrity.

Session management in SPAs is another important aspect of OIDC integration. Unlike traditional web applications that rely on server-side sessions, SPAs manage sessions on the client side using tokens. The lifespan of an access token is typically short to reduce the risk of misuse, but SPAs can use refresh tokens to maintain long-lived sessions without requiring the user to re-authenticate frequently. However, refresh tokens introduce additional security risks if not handled properly. OIDC specifies that refresh tokens should be securely stored and transmitted, and their use should be limited to prevent abuse. For SPAs, this often means leveraging secure HTTP-only cookies or other secure storage mechanisms provided by the browser.

The user interface plays a significant role in the authentication flow of SPAs. Redirecting users to an external browser or a popup window for authentication is a common practice that enhances security by isolating the authentication process from the main application. This prevents the SPA from directly handling user credentials, reducing the risk of credential exposure. After successful authentication, the identity provider redirects the user back to the application with the authorization code, which the application then exchanges for tokens. This process, while secure, must be carefully implemented to provide a smooth and intuitive user experience, avoiding disruptions or confusing transitions.

Error handling and user feedback are essential components of a robust OIDC implementation in SPAs. Applications should be designed to gracefully handle scenarios where authentication fails, tokens expire, or network connectivity is lost. Providing clear, actionable messages helps users understand and resolve issues, maintaining trust and satisfaction. Additionally, logging and monitoring authentication activities can help developers identify potential security threats or performance bottlenecks, ensuring the application remains secure and responsive.

OIDC also facilitates compliance with data protection regulations and industry standards in SPA development. By adhering to standardized authentication protocols and implementing secure token management practices, developers can ensure that their applications meet legal and regulatory requirements, such as the General Data Protection Regulation (GDPR) or the California Consumer Privacy Act (CCPA). This is particularly important in applications that handle sensitive user data, where protecting privacy and maintaining trust are paramount.

In summary, integrating OpenID Connect into Single Page Applications provides a secure, standardized approach to user authentication and identity management. By leveraging the Authorization Code Flow with PKCE, SPAs can protect against common security threats, manage tokens securely, and deliver seamless, personalized user experiences. As SPAs continue to evolve and become more prevalent in web development, OIDC will remain a critical tool for ensuring that these applications are both secure and user-friendly, supporting the growing demand for dynamic, responsive digital experiences.

Integrating OIDC with Native Applications

OpenID Connect (OIDC) has become an essential protocol for secure user authentication and authorization across a wide variety of platforms, including native applications. Native applications, which run directly on user devices such as desktops, smartphones, and tablets, present unique challenges when it comes to securely managing authentication flows. Unlike web applications, which benefit from secure server environments, native apps often operate in less controlled environments, making them more susceptible to security vulnerabilities. Integrating OIDC into native applications addresses these challenges by providing a standardized, robust, and secure method for handling authentication.

One of the key considerations in integrating OIDC with native applications is selecting the appropriate authentication flow. The Authorization Code Flow with Proof Key for Code Exchange (PKCE) is the recommended flow for native applications. This flow enhances security by preventing authorization code interception attacks, a common risk in environments where client secrets cannot be securely stored. The PKCE extension introduces an additional verification step that ensures the authorization code, even if intercepted, cannot be used without the original code verifier.

The process begins when the native application generates a random code verifier and creates a code challenge by applying a cryptographic hash function, typically SHA-256, to the verifier. The application then initiates an authentication request by redirecting the user to the identity provider's authorization endpoint, including the code challenge in the request parameters. After the user authenticates and grants the requested permissions, the identity provider redirects them back to the application with an authorization code. To exchange this code for tokens, the application must present the original code verifier to the identity provider's token endpoint. The identity provider hashes the code verifier and compares it to the code challenge from the initial request. If they match, the tokens are issued, ensuring that only the legitimate application can complete the process.

Another critical aspect of integrating OIDC with native applications is handling the redirection and token retrieval process securely. Native applications typically use custom URI schemes or platform-specific mechanisms like Android App Links or iOS Universal Links to handle redirections. These mechanisms ensure that the authorization response is securely delivered to the correct application without exposing sensitive information to unauthorized apps. It is essential to register these URI schemes properly and implement strict validation to prevent unauthorized interception.

Once the tokens are received, secure storage and management become paramount. Native applications should use secure storage mechanisms provided by the operating system, such as the iOS Keychain or Android's EncryptedSharedPreferences, to protect tokens from unauthorized access. Storing tokens in plain text or insecure locations can expose them to malicious actors, compromising the application's security. Additionally, applications should implement proper token expiration and refresh strategies to maintain secure and seamless user sessions. Access tokens are typically short-lived, and refresh tokens can be used to obtain new access tokens without requiring the user to re-authenticate.

Integrating OIDC with native applications also involves careful management of user sessions and handling of potential errors. Applications should implement robust session management strategies, including token revocation and logout mechanisms. When a user logs out of the application, it is crucial to clear all stored tokens and notify the identity provider to invalidate any active sessions. This prevents unauthorized access if the device is lost or shared with others. Additionally, handling errors gracefully, such as expired tokens or network failures, enhances the user experience and ensures that authentication processes remain reliable and secure.

Security best practices extend beyond token management to include the secure handling of sensitive user information. OIDC allows applications to request specific scopes and claims, defining the level of access and the information returned by the identity provider. Applications should request only the necessary scopes to minimize data exposure and adhere to the principle of least privilege. For instance, if an application only requires basic profile information, it should limit its request to the openid and profile scopes, avoiding unnecessary access to more sensitive data like email or phone numbers.

The user experience in native applications can also benefit significantly from OIDC integration. Single Sign-On (SSO) capabilities allow users to authenticate once and access multiple applications without repeated logins. This seamless experience is achieved by leveraging shared identity providers and maintaining consistent session states across applications. Native applications can integrate with popular identity providers such as Google, Microsoft, or enterprise identity solutions to offer users a familiar and convenient authentication process.

In federated identity scenarios, native applications can further simplify user management by allowing users to authenticate using their existing credentials from trusted external identity providers. This approach reduces the need for users to create and manage multiple accounts while enabling organizations to maintain control over authentication policies and security measures. By integrating OIDC with federated identity systems, native applications can provide a unified and secure authentication experience across diverse platforms and services.

Developers integrating OIDC into native applications should also consider the implications of cross-platform development. Applications built using frameworks like React Native, Xamarin, or Flutter need to ensure that their OIDC implementations are consistent and secure across different operating systems. Leveraging platform-specific libraries and SDKs that support OIDC and PKCE can simplify the development process and ensure compliance with best practices. These libraries often provide built-in methods for handling token management, secure storage, and redirection, reducing the complexity of implementing OIDC from scratch.

Testing and monitoring are critical components of a successful OIDC integration in native applications. Developers should rigorously test authentication flows, error handling, and security mechanisms to identify and address potential vulnerabilities. Continuous monitoring of authentication events, token usage, and user sessions can help detect suspicious activities and ensure the integrity of the authentication process. Implementing logging and auditing features can also aid in troubleshooting and maintaining compliance with security and privacy regulations.

Regulatory compliance is another important consideration when integrating OIDC with native applications. Depending on the application's domain, developers may need to adhere to specific regulations such as GDPR, HIPAA, or PCI-DSS. OIDC's standardized protocols and secure handling of identity information help meet these regulatory requirements, but developers must ensure that their implementation aligns with the relevant legal and security standards. This includes obtaining user consent for data access, implementing data minimization practices, and ensuring secure data transmission and storage.

In summary, integrating OpenID Connect with native applications provides a secure, standardized framework for handling user authentication and identity management. By leveraging the Authorization Code Flow with PKCE, secure token storage, and best practices for session management, developers can create robust and user-friendly applications that protect sensitive information and enhance the user experience. As native applications continue to evolve and play a central role in the digital landscape, OIDC will remain a vital tool for ensuring secure and seamless authentication across diverse platforms and devices.

OIDC and API Security

OpenID Connect (OIDC), built on top of the OAuth 2.0 framework, has become a cornerstone for modern identity management and secure API interactions. As APIs play a crucial role in powering web, mobile, and enterprise applications, securing these interfaces is vital to protect sensitive data and maintain system integrity. OIDC enhances API security by providing a standardized mechanism for authenticating users and services, issuing tokens, and ensuring that only authorized entities can access protected resources.

At the heart of OIDC's role in API security is the use of tokens— specifically, the ID token, access token, and refresh token. While the ID token is primarily used for authenticating users and conveying identity information to client applications, the access token is the critical component that APIs rely on to control access to their endpoints. When a client application requests access to an API, it must include a valid access token in the authorization header of its HTTP requests. The API, acting as the resource server, then verifies the token to ensure the request is legitimate and that the client has the appropriate permissions to perform the requested action.

Access tokens are typically formatted as JSON Web Tokens (JWTs), which are compact, URL-safe tokens that include claims about the token's issuer, audience, expiration time, and the scopes of access granted. These tokens are signed by the identity provider to prevent tampering, and the API can verify the signature using the public key provided by the identity provider's JSON Web Key Set (JWKS) endpoint. This process of token validation ensures that only tokens issued by trusted identity providers are accepted and that the integrity of the token's contents is maintained.

One of the key security features of OIDC in API interactions is the concept of scopes. Scopes define the level of access that the client application is requesting from the API. For example, an application might request the read:profile scope to retrieve user profile information or the write:settings scope to modify user settings. By specifying scopes in the access token, OIDC allows APIs to enforce fine-grained access control, ensuring that clients can only perform actions they have explicitly been granted permission for. This granular control helps prevent unauthorized access and limits the potential impact of compromised tokens.

To further enhance API security, OIDC supports the use of claims within tokens. Claims provide additional context about the authenticated user or client, such as their unique identifier (sub), roles, or other attributes relevant to access control decisions. APIs can leverage these claims to implement role-based access control (RBAC) or attribute-based access control (ABAC), granting or restricting access based on the user's identity and associated attributes. This flexibility allows APIs to enforce complex security policies and tailor access permissions to specific use cases.

Another important aspect of securing APIs with OIDC is the management of token lifecycles. Access tokens are typically short-lived, with expiration times designed to minimize the window of opportunity for token misuse if compromised. When an access token expires, the client application must obtain a new one, either by prompting the user to re-authenticate or by using a refresh token if available. Refresh tokens are long-lived tokens that allow clients to obtain new access tokens without requiring user interaction. However, because refresh tokens provide extended access, they must be handled with care, stored securely, and protected against unauthorized access.

To protect against token replay attacks, where an attacker intercepts a token and attempts to reuse it, APIs should implement mechanisms to validate the token's audience (aud) and issuer (iss) claims. The audience claim ensures that the token is intended for the specific API, while the issuer claim verifies that the token was issued by a trusted identity provider. Additionally, implementing token binding, where tokens are tied to specific client instances or devices, can further reduce the risk of token misuse by ensuring that tokens cannot be used outside of their intended context.

Securing APIs with OIDC also involves safeguarding the communication channels through which tokens and API requests are transmitted. All interactions between clients, identity providers, and APIs should be conducted over secure HTTPS connections to protect against eavesdropping and man-in-the-middle attacks. Moreover, APIs should employ rate limiting, logging, and monitoring to detect and respond to suspicious activity, such as repeated failed authentication attempts or unusual patterns of API usage.

In federated identity scenarios, where multiple organizations or domains share authentication infrastructure, OIDC facilitates secure API interactions across organizational boundaries. By establishing trust relationships between identity providers and APIs, federated systems can ensure that tokens issued by external identity providers are accepted and validated correctly. This capability is essential for enabling secure collaboration between partners, suppliers, and customers, allowing APIs to serve diverse user bases while maintaining stringent security standards.

The adoption of OIDC for API security also supports compliance with industry standards and regulatory requirements. By leveraging a standardized authentication protocol, organizations can ensure that their API security practices align with best practices for data protection and privacy. OIDC's support for multi-factor authentication (MFA), secure token storage, and fine-grained access control helps organizations meet the security requirements of frameworks such as GDPR, HIPAA, and PCI-DSS.

In modern microservices architectures, where applications are composed of numerous interconnected services, OIDC plays a critical role in securing service-to-service communication. By issuing and validating tokens for inter-service API calls, OIDC ensures that each service can authenticate and authorize requests from other services securely. This approach not only protects sensitive data but also enforces consistent security policies across the entire application ecosystem, reducing the risk of unauthorized access and data breaches.

Implementing OIDC for API security requires careful planning and adherence to best practices. Developers must ensure that access tokens are properly validated, that scopes and claims are used effectively to control access, and that tokens are stored and transmitted securely. Regular security assessments, code reviews, and penetration testing can help identify and address potential vulnerabilities, ensuring that APIs remain secure in the face of evolving threats.

As the digital landscape continues to evolve, the importance of securing APIs with robust, standardized authentication mechanisms like OIDC cannot be overstated. By providing a comprehensive framework for user and service authentication, token management, and access control, OIDC empowers organizations to protect their APIs, safeguard sensitive data, and build trust with users and partners. Through careful implementation and ongoing vigilance, OIDC helps create secure, resilient API ecosystems that support the growing demands of modern digital applications.

Best Practices for Token Storage and Management

In modern authentication systems, especially those leveraging OAuth 2.0 and OpenID Connect (OIDC), tokens play a crucial role in securing communication and maintaining user sessions. Tokens, including access tokens, ID tokens, and refresh tokens, grant clients access to protected resources and convey essential user identity information. However, improper storage and management of these tokens can lead to severe security vulnerabilities, including unauthorized access, data breaches, and compromised user privacy. Understanding and implementing best practices for token storage and management is vital to ensuring the security and integrity of any application that relies on token-based authentication.

Tokens are sensitive pieces of data that act as keys to access user information and services. If intercepted or improperly handled, tokens can be exploited by malicious actors to impersonate users or gain unauthorized access to resources. This makes it essential to store tokens securely, both in transit and at rest. For web applications, especially Single Page Applications (SPAs), tokens should never be stored in insecure locations like local storage or session storage. These storage mechanisms are vulnerable to cross-site scripting (XSS) attacks, where malicious scripts injected into a webpage can read and exfiltrate tokens stored in the browser's storage.

Instead, tokens should be stored in memory within the application, ensuring that they are only accessible during the active session and cleared when the user logs out or closes the browser. While this approach minimizes the risk of token theft, it requires careful session management to handle token expiration and renewal. Applications should be designed to detect when tokens expire and prompt the user to re-authenticate or silently renew tokens using secure methods, such as refresh tokens.

Refresh tokens, which allow applications to obtain new access tokens without requiring the user to log in again, introduce additional security considerations. Because refresh tokens typically have longer lifespans than access tokens, their compromise poses a significant risk. For SPAs and mobile applications, storing refresh tokens in secure, HTTP-only cookies is recommended. These cookies are inaccessible to JavaScript, reducing the risk of XSS attacks, and can be configured with attributes like Secure and SameSite to protect against man-in-the-middle and cross-site request forgery (CSRF) attacks.

For mobile applications, platform-specific secure storage solutions should be used to protect tokens. On iOS devices, the Keychain provides a secure environment for storing sensitive data, while Android offers EncryptedSharedPreferences and the Android Keystore system for secure token storage. These mechanisms encrypt data at rest and protect it with device-level security, such as biometric authentication or passcodes, ensuring that tokens remain secure even if the device is compromised.

In server-side applications, where tokens are stored on the backend, developers have more control over security measures. Access and refresh tokens should be stored in encrypted databases or secure storage services, with access restricted to authorized processes only. Additionally, token storage should be accompanied by strict access controls and logging to monitor and detect any unauthorized access attempts. Regularly rotating encryption keys and using strong encryption algorithms further enhances the security of stored tokens.

Securing tokens in transit is equally important as securing them at rest. All token exchanges between clients and servers should occur over secure communication channels, such as HTTPS, to protect against eavesdropping and man-in-the-middle attacks. Implementing certificate pinning can add an extra layer of security by ensuring that the application only communicates with trusted servers. Furthermore, tokens should be scoped to the minimum permissions required for the application's functionality, following the principle of least privilege. This limits the potential damage if a token is compromised.

Token expiration and revocation are critical aspects of token lifecycle management. Access tokens should have short expiration times to reduce the window of opportunity for misuse if they are intercepted. When tokens expire, applications should use refresh tokens to obtain new access tokens securely. However, if a refresh token is suspected to be compromised, it should be revoked immediately, and the user should be prompted to re-authenticate. Implementing token revocation endpoints allows administrators to invalidate tokens manually, providing an additional layer of control over access management.

Monitoring and logging token usage is another best practice that helps detect suspicious activity and respond to potential security threats. Applications should log token issuance, usage, and revocation events, along with relevant metadata such as timestamps, IP addresses, and device identifiers. Analyzing these logs can reveal patterns indicative of unauthorized access attempts, such as multiple failed token exchanges or token usage from unexpected locations. Integrating monitoring tools and setting up alerts for anomalous behavior enables proactive security management.

To further protect token integrity, applications should validate tokens on every request. This includes verifying the token's signature to ensure it was issued by a trusted identity provider, checking the token's expiration time, and confirming that the token's audience (aud) and issuer (iss) claims match the expected values. For access tokens used to secure APIs, the resource server should enforce these validations to prevent unauthorized access.

Adopting a zero-trust approach to token management is also beneficial. This security model assumes that no token or session is inherently trustworthy, requiring continuous verification of user identity and token validity. Implementing multi-factor authentication (MFA) adds an extra layer of security by requiring users to provide additional verification factors beyond just a token. This approach reduces the risk of unauthorized access even if a token is compromised.

Regularly updating and patching dependencies related to authentication and token management is crucial to maintaining security. Vulnerabilities in libraries or frameworks can expose applications to token-related attacks, such as token leakage or improper validation. Keeping software up to date with the latest security patches and following the best practices recommended by the OIDC and OAuth 2.0 specifications ensures that applications remain resilient against evolving threats.

Education and awareness are fundamental components of secure token management. Developers and administrators should be trained on the principles of secure token handling, common attack vectors, and mitigation strategies. Regular security audits, code reviews, and penetration testing help identify weaknesses in token management practices and provide opportunities for continuous improvement.

In summary, secure token storage and management are essential for protecting user data and maintaining the integrity of authentication systems. By implementing best practices such as using secure storage mechanisms, enforcing strict access controls, validating tokens, and monitoring usage, applications can safeguard tokens against compromise and ensure secure, reliable user authentication. As the digital landscape continues to evolve, staying vigilant and proactive in token management remains a critical aspect of maintaining robust security in modern applications.

Implementing OIDC in Java Applications

OpenID Connect (OIDC) provides a simple, flexible, and secure method for user authentication and identity management across various platforms, and its integration into Java applications is both robust and scalable. Java, as one of the most widely used programming languages, supports OIDC through a variety of libraries and frameworks, allowing developers to implement secure authentication mechanisms in web, mobile, and enterprise applications. Leveraging OIDC in Java not only enhances security but also simplifies the management of user identities, access tokens, and session states.

To begin implementing OIDC in a Java application, the first step is to select an appropriate library or framework that supports OIDC protocols. Popular choices include Spring Security, which provides extensive support for OAuth 2.0 and OIDC, and libraries like Nimbus JOSE + JWT for handling JSON Web Tokens (JWT). These libraries abstract much of the complexity involved in authentication flows, token validation, and secure communication, making it easier for developers to integrate OIDC into their applications.

Spring Security, in particular, is a powerful framework for securing Java applications and offers comprehensive support for OIDC. By leveraging Spring Security's OAuth 2.0 Client and Resource Server capabilities, developers can implement OIDC authentication flows such as the Authorization Code Flow with Proof Key for Code Exchange (PKCE), which is recommended for most applications due to its enhanced security features. The Authorization Code Flow with PKCE protects against authorization code interception attacks, ensuring that only legitimate clients can exchange authorization codes for tokens.

Configuring OIDC in a Spring Boot application involves several steps. First, you need to add the necessary dependencies to your pom.xml file if you are using Maven. This typically includes the spring-boot-starter-oauth2-client and spring-boot-starter-security dependencies. Once the dependencies are in place, you can configure your application's application.properties or application.yml file with the details of your OIDC provider, such as the issuer URI, client ID, and client secret. These configurations allow your application to communicate with the identity provider and handle authentication requests.

For example, a basic configuration in application.yml might look like this:

```
spring:

  security:

   oauth2:

    client:

     registration:

      my-oidc-provider:

       client-id: your-client-id

       client-secret: your-client-secret

       scope: openid, profile, email

       redirect-uri: "{baseUrl}/login/oauth2/code/{registrationId}"

       authorization-grant-type: authorization_code

       client-name: OIDC Provider
```

```
provider:

  my-oidc-provider:

    issuer-uri: https://your-oidc-provider.com
```

This configuration sets up the necessary parameters for your Java application to authenticate users via OIDC. The issuer-uri points to the OIDC provider's discovery endpoint, allowing the application to retrieve metadata such as authorization and token endpoints, supported scopes, and public keys for token validation.

Once the configuration is complete, Spring Security automatically handles the redirection of users to the identity provider's login page, the processing of authorization codes, and the exchange for access and ID tokens. The ID token contains claims about the authenticated user, such as their unique identifier (sub), name, and email address, which can be accessed within the application to personalize the user experience or enforce authorization rules.

Token validation is a critical aspect of OIDC implementation in Java applications. Spring Security handles much of the token validation process automatically, including verifying the token's signature, checking its expiration time, and ensuring that the token's audience (aud) matches the expected value. However, in some cases, developers may need to implement custom validation logic, such as additional checks on specific claims or integrating with external authorization services.

In applications that expose APIs or need to secure resource servers, the spring-boot-starter-oauth2-resource-server dependency can be used to protect endpoints and validate access tokens. By configuring the resource server with the OIDC provider's public keys and expected token claims, you can ensure that only authenticated and authorized clients can access protected resources.

For applications that require more granular control over authentication flows, libraries like Nimbus JOSE + JWT provide low-level tools for handling JWTs, signing and verifying tokens, and managing cryptographic keys. This library is particularly useful for custom implementations or when integrating OIDC into non-Spring Java applications.

Beyond basic authentication, OIDC integration in Java applications supports advanced features such as Single Sign-On (SSO) and federated identity management. By configuring multiple identity providers and supporting federated login, Java applications can offer seamless authentication experiences across different domains and services. This is particularly valuable in enterprise environments where users need to access a variety of applications with a single set of credentials.

Session management is another important consideration when implementing OIDC in Java applications. Spring Security provides tools for managing user sessions, including automatic token renewal using refresh tokens, session timeout configurations, and secure session storage. Proper session management ensures that users remain authenticated without frequent disruptions while maintaining the security of active sessions.

Security best practices should be followed throughout the OIDC implementation process. This includes using secure communication channels (HTTPS) for all interactions with the identity provider, protecting client secrets in configuration files, and implementing logging and monitoring to detect and respond to authentication-related security events. Regular security assessments and code reviews help identify potential vulnerabilities and ensure that the application remains secure against evolving threats.

In summary, implementing OpenID Connect in Java applications provides a secure and standardized approach to user authentication and identity management. By leveraging frameworks like Spring Security and libraries such as Nimbus JOSE + JWT, developers can integrate robust authentication mechanisms, manage tokens securely, and deliver seamless user experiences. Whether building web applications, securing APIs, or enabling federated identity, OIDC offers the flexibility and security needed to meet the demands of modern Java development.

OIDC Integration with .NET Applications

OpenID Connect (OIDC) is an identity layer built on top of the OAuth 2.0 protocol that provides a standardized framework for authenticating users and securely transmitting identity information. Integrating OIDC into .NET applications allows developers to leverage this robust protocol to manage authentication, user identity, and secure access to resources in a consistent manner. With the widespread adoption of .NET for developing web applications, APIs, and enterprise solutions, understanding how to effectively implement OIDC within this ecosystem is critical for maintaining strong security practices and delivering seamless user experiences.

The foundation of OIDC integration in .NET applications lies in the use of the Microsoft Identity platform and libraries such as Microsoft.Identity.Web and OpenIdConnect middleware in ASP.NET Core. These tools simplify the process of implementing OIDC, allowing developers to focus on building application logic while relying on standardized authentication flows and secure token management.

The first step in integrating OIDC into a .NET application is registering the application with an identity provider, such as Azure Active Directory (Azure AD), Autho, or another OIDC-compliant provider. This registration process generates essential configuration details, including the client ID, client secret, and redirect URIs. The client ID uniquely identifies the application, while the client secret, in confidential client scenarios, is used to authenticate the application with the identity provider. Redirect URIs specify where the identity provider should send authentication responses, ensuring that tokens are delivered to trusted endpoints within the application.

Once the application is registered, developers can configure the .NET application to use OIDC for authentication. In ASP.NET Core applications, this typically involves adding the OpenIdConnect middleware to the application's authentication pipeline. This middleware handles the OIDC protocol flow, including redirecting users to the identity provider for authentication, handling the response, and managing tokens. Configuration settings such as the authority (the identity provider's URL), client ID, client secret, and scopes are specified in the application's settings file, often appsettings.json, and injected into the middleware during startup.

The Authorization Code Flow with Proof Key for Code Exchange (PKCE) is the recommended authentication flow for .NET applications, particularly for public clients like desktop applications or single-page applications (SPAs). This flow enhances security by adding an additional verification step that prevents authorization code interception attacks. During the authentication process, the application generates a code verifier and transforms it into a code challenge. The code challenge is sent to the identity provider during the authorization request, and the code verifier is used later to securely exchange the authorization code for tokens.

Tokens issued by the identity provider include the ID token, access token, and optionally, a refresh token. The ID token contains claims about the authenticated user, such as their unique identifier (sub), name, and email address. This token is used by the .NET application to establish the user's identity and manage session state. The access token grants the application permission to access protected resources, such as APIs or other backend services, on behalf of the user. Refresh tokens, if issued, allow the application to obtain new access tokens without requiring the user to re-authenticate, supporting long-lived sessions and enhancing user experience.

Proper token handling and validation are critical components of secure OIDC integration. The .NET application must validate the ID token to ensure it was issued by a trusted identity provider and has not been tampered with. This validation process includes verifying the token's signature, checking the expiration time, and ensuring that the aud (audience) and iss (issuer) claims match the expected values. Microsoft.Identity.Web and related libraries provide built-in methods for token validation, simplifying this process and ensuring compliance with best practices.

Securing tokens at rest and in transit is essential to protect against unauthorized access and potential security breaches. In server-side .NET applications, tokens should be stored securely in encrypted databases or secure session stores. For desktop applications, secure storage mechanisms provided by the operating system, such as the

Windows Credential Manager, should be used. All communication involving tokens, including token requests and API calls, must be conducted over secure HTTPS channels to protect against eavesdropping and man-in-the-middle attacks.

Role-based access control (RBAC) and claim-based authorization are powerful features enabled by OIDC integration in .NET applications. By leveraging the claims included in the ID token, such as roles or group memberships, applications can implement fine-grained access control policies that restrict or grant access to specific resources based on the user's identity and permissions. ASP.NET Core's built-in authorization framework allows developers to define policies and apply them to controllers, actions, or entire areas of the application, ensuring that sensitive operations are protected and only accessible to authorized users.

Single Sign-On (SSO) capabilities are another significant benefit of integrating OIDC with .NET applications. SSO allows users to authenticate once with an identity provider and gain access to multiple applications without needing to log in repeatedly. This seamless experience enhances user productivity and reduces the burden of managing multiple credentials. In enterprise environments, integrating with Azure AD or other federated identity providers enables SSO across a wide range of internal and external applications, streamlining access management and improving security.

In scenarios where .NET applications act as APIs or resource servers, OIDC plays a crucial role in securing API endpoints. APIs can be configured to accept access tokens issued by the identity provider, validating these tokens on each request to ensure that the caller is authenticated and authorized. The Microsoft.AspNetCore.Authentication.JwtBearer middleware facilitates this process by automatically handling token validation and enforcing authorization policies based on the claims present in the access token. This approach ensures that APIs are protected against unauthorized access and that only authenticated clients with appropriate permissions can interact with the API.

Integrating OIDC with .NET applications also supports compliance with industry standards and regulatory requirements. By adhering to standardized authentication protocols and implementing secure token management practices, organizations can meet security and privacy requirements for frameworks such as GDPR, HIPAA, and PCI-DSS. OIDC's support for multi-factor authentication (MFA), secure token storage, and audit logging further enhances compliance efforts, ensuring that sensitive data is protected and that authentication processes are transparent and auditable.

In summary, integrating OpenID Connect with .NET applications provides a secure, standardized framework for managing user authentication and authorization. By leveraging the Microsoft Identity platform, OpenIdConnect middleware, and best practices for token handling and validation, developers can create robust applications that protect user identities, secure access to resources, and deliver seamless authentication experiences. As the digital landscape continues to evolve, OIDC will remain a vital tool for securing .NET applications and ensuring that identity management practices align with modern security standards and user expectations.

Using OIDC in Python and Flask/Django

OpenID Connect (OIDC) is a widely adopted protocol for identity management and secure user authentication, built on top of the OAuth 2.0 framework. Python, as a versatile and popular programming language, offers robust support for OIDC integration, particularly through its leading web frameworks, Flask and Django. Both frameworks provide powerful tools for building web applications, and integrating OIDC into these frameworks enhances security, simplifies user authentication, and streamlines identity management.

When integrating OIDC into Python applications, developers benefit from a variety of libraries designed to simplify the authentication process. Libraries such as authlib, python-jose, and django-oidc-provider provide comprehensive support for OIDC, including handling token exchanges, validating tokens, and securing user sessions. These libraries abstract much of the complexity of OIDC, allowing developers to focus on building application features while ensuring robust authentication and security practices.

In Flask applications, the authlib library is a popular choice for implementing OIDC. Authlib provides a flexible and easy-to-use interface for integrating OAuth 2.0 and OIDC authentication flows. To get started with OIDC in a Flask application, you first need to install authlib using pip:

pip install Authlib

Once installed, you can configure your Flask application to use an OIDC provider. The configuration involves setting up the client ID, client secret, and the discovery URL provided by the OIDC provider. The discovery URL allows the application to automatically retrieve metadata about the provider, including endpoints for authorization, token exchange, and user information.

Here is an example of how to configure OIDC in a Flask application using authlib:

```
from flask import Flask, redirect, url_for, session

from authlib.integrations.flask_client import OAuth

app = Flask(__name__)

app.secret_key = 'your_secret_key'

oauth = OAuth(app)

oidc = oauth.register(

    name='oidc',

    client_id='your_client_id',

    client_secret='your_client_secret',

    server_metadata_url='https://your-oidc-provider.com/.well-known/openid-configuration',

    client_kwargs={
```

```python
        'scope': 'openid profile email'

    }

)

@app.route('/')

def homepage():

    user = session.get('user')

    if user:

        return f"Hello, {user['name']}!"

    return 'Welcome! <a href="/login">Login</a>'

@app.route('/login')

def login():

    redirect_uri = url_for('authorize', _external=True)

    return oidc.authorize_redirect(redirect_uri)

@app.route('/authorize')

def authorize():

    token = oidc.authorize_access_token()

    user_info = oidc.parse_id_token(token)

    session['user'] = user_info

    return redirect('/')

@app.route('/logout')
```

```
def logout():

    session.pop('user', None)

    return redirect('/')
```

In this example, the application redirects the user to the OIDC provider's login page when they access the /login route. After successful authentication, the provider redirects the user back to the application's /authorize route, where the application exchanges the authorization code for tokens and retrieves user information from the ID token. The user's information is stored in the session, allowing the application to personalize the user experience.

Django, as a more structured and feature-rich framework, offers its own set of tools for OIDC integration. The mozilla-django-oidc library is a popular choice for adding OIDC authentication to Django applications. This library simplifies the process of configuring OIDC providers, handling authentication flows, and managing user sessions.

To integrate OIDC in a Django application, start by installing the mozilla-django-oidc package:

pip install mozilla-django-oidc

Next, add mozilla_django_oidc to your INSTALLED_APPS in the settings.py file and configure the OIDC settings:

INSTALLED_APPS = [

    ...

    'mozilla_django_oidc',

]

AUTHENTICATION_BACKENDS = (

    'mozilla_django_oidc.auth.OIDCAuthenticationBackend',

```
    'django.contrib.auth.backends.ModelBackend',

)

OIDC_RP_CLIENT_ID = 'your_client_id'

OIDC_RP_CLIENT_SECRET = 'your_client_secret'

OIDC_OP_AUTHORIZATION_ENDPOINT   =   'https://your-oidc-
provider.com/authorize'

OIDC_OP_TOKEN_ENDPOINT           =           'https://your-oidc-
provider.com/token'

OIDC_OP_USER_ENDPOINT            =           'https://your-oidc-
provider.com/userinfo'

OIDC_OP_JWKS_ENDPOINT            =           'https://your-oidc-
provider.com/.well-known/jwks.json'

LOGIN_URL = '/oidc/authenticate/'

LOGIN_REDIRECT_URL = '/'

LOGOUT_REDIRECT_URL = '/'
```

With these settings in place, Django's built-in authentication views are extended to support OIDC. Users can authenticate via the OIDC provider by navigating to the /oidc/authenticate/ route, and upon successful login, they are redirected to the specified LOGIN_REDIRECT_URL. The library handles token validation, session management, and user information retrieval, allowing developers to focus on building application features.

Security is a critical consideration when integrating OIDC into Flask and Django applications. Both frameworks offer tools and best practices for securing tokens, managing user sessions, and protecting against common web vulnerabilities. For example, secure token storage is essential to prevent unauthorized access. In Flask, tokens should be stored in secure, HTTP-only cookies or session variables, while Django's session framework provides robust mechanisms for managing session data securely.

Additionally, both frameworks support middleware and decorators for protecting routes and enforcing access control. In Flask, you can use decorators to restrict access to authenticated users:

```python
from functools import wraps

from flask import redirect, url_for, session

def login_required(f):

    @wraps(f)

    def decorated_function(*args, **kwargs):

        if 'user' not in session:

            return redirect(url_for('login'))

        return f(*args, **kwargs)

    return decorated_function

@app.route('/protected')

@login_required

def protected():

    return 'This is a protected route.'
```

In Django, the @login_required decorator from django.contrib.auth.decorators can be used to achieve similar functionality:

```python
from django.contrib.auth.decorators import login_required

from django.shortcuts import render
```

```
@login_required

def protected_view(request):

    return render(request, 'protected.html')
```

Integrating OIDC in Python applications using Flask and Django not only simplifies user authentication but also enhances the overall security and user experience. By leveraging OIDC's standardized protocols and robust libraries, developers can build secure, scalable applications that provide seamless access to users while protecting sensitive data. As identity management continues to evolve, OIDC remains a critical tool in the Python developer's toolkit, enabling secure and efficient authentication across diverse application environments.

OIDC for Node.js Applications

OpenID Connect (OIDC) is an identity layer built on top of the OAuth 2.0 protocol, providing a secure, standardized method for user authentication and identity management across web, mobile, and enterprise applications. Node.js, a popular JavaScript runtime environment, is widely used for building scalable, high-performance applications, and integrating OIDC into Node.js applications allows developers to implement robust authentication mechanisms while maintaining streamlined codebases. This chapter explores how to effectively implement OIDC in Node.js applications, ensuring secure user authentication and seamless access control.

To begin integrating OIDC into a Node.js application, it is essential to select the appropriate libraries that facilitate OIDC and OAuth 2.0 protocols. One of the most popular and comprehensive libraries for handling OIDC in Node.js is passport-openidconnect, a strategy for the Passport.js authentication middleware. Passport.js is a flexible and modular authentication middleware for Node.js, supporting various authentication mechanisms, including OIDC, OAuth 2.0, and SAML. Another widely used library is openid-client, which offers a more direct interface for managing OIDC flows without relying on Passport's abstraction.

Setting up OIDC in a Node.js application typically begins with registering the application with an identity provider, such as Autho, Okta, or Google Identity. This registration process generates critical configuration information, including the client ID, client secret, redirect URIs, and the discovery endpoint URL of the identity provider. The client ID uniquely identifies the application, while the client secret authenticates confidential clients during the token exchange process. The redirect URI specifies where the identity provider sends the authentication response after the user has successfully logged in.

Once the application is registered, the next step is to configure the Node.js application to use OIDC for authentication. If using passport-openidconnect, the configuration involves setting up the OIDC strategy with the required parameters. This includes specifying the issuer, client ID, client secret, callback URL, and scopes. The scopes define the level of access the application is requesting, such as openid for basic identity information, profile for user profile details, and email for the user's email address.

A sample configuration using passport-openidconnect might look like this:

```
const passport = require('passport');

const { Strategy } = require('passport-openidconnect');

passport.use('oidc', new Strategy({

  issuer: 'https://your-identity-provider.com',

  clientID: 'your-client-id',

  clientSecret: 'your-client-secret',

  authorizationURL: 'https://your-identity-provider.com/authorize',

  tokenURL: 'https://your-identity-provider.com/token',

  userInfoURL: 'https://your-identity-provider.com/userinfo',
```

```
callbackURL: 'http://localhost:3000/auth/callback',

scope: 'openid profile email'

}, (issuer, sub, profile, accessToken, refreshToken, done) => {

return done(null, profile);

}));
```

This configuration initializes the OIDC strategy, enabling the Node.js application to redirect users to the identity provider for authentication and handle the response upon successful login. The callback function processes the user profile and tokens, allowing the application to establish the user's identity and manage session state.

For developers seeking a more granular approach, the openid-client library provides a lower-level API for handling OIDC flows. This library allows for greater control over token management, discovery, and validation processes. To use openid-client, developers first create an OIDC client by discovering the identity provider's configuration from the well-known discovery endpoint.

Here's an example using openid-client:

```
const { Issuer } = require('openid-client');

async function setupOIDC() {

  const oidcIssuer = await Issuer.discover('https://your-identity-provider.com');

  const client = new oidcIssuer.Client({

    client_id: 'your-client-id',

    client_secret: 'your-client-secret',

    redirect_uris: ['http://localhost:3000/callback'],
```

```
    response_types: ['code']

  });

  return client;

}
```

This setup retrieves the identity provider's metadata, including authorization, token, and user info endpoints, and initializes the client with the necessary credentials and redirect URIs.

Securing tokens in Node.js applications is a critical aspect of OIDC integration. Access tokens, ID tokens, and refresh tokens must be stored securely to prevent unauthorized access and token theft. In server-side applications, tokens should be stored in secure server sessions or encrypted databases. For APIs or microservices, tokens can be passed in the Authorization header of HTTP requests, and validated on each request to ensure that only authenticated users can access protected resources.

Token validation is a fundamental part of securing OIDC-based applications. Node.js applications must verify the ID token's signature using the public key provided by the identity provider's JSON Web Key Set (JWKS) endpoint. This ensures the token was issued by a trusted source and has not been tampered with. Additionally, the application should check the token's expiration time, issuer (iss), audience (aud), and other claims to confirm that the token is valid for the intended purpose.

Session management in Node.js applications can be handled using packages like express-session, which stores session data on the server side and uses cookies to manage session IDs. When combined with OIDC, session management involves storing user information and tokens in the session after successful authentication. This allows the application to maintain the user's authenticated state across multiple requests without repeatedly prompting for login.

Implementing Single Sign-On (SSO) capabilities in Node.js applications is another significant advantage of OIDC integration. SSO allows users to authenticate once with an identity provider and access multiple applications without repeated logins. This seamless experience enhances user productivity and simplifies identity management in environments where multiple applications rely on the same authentication infrastructure.

For APIs and microservices built with Node.js, OIDC facilitates secure, token-based access control. APIs can be configured to accept access tokens from trusted identity providers, using middleware like express-jwt or passport-jwt to validate tokens on incoming requests. This ensures that only authenticated and authorized clients can interact with the API, protecting sensitive data and enforcing access control policies.

In federated identity scenarios, Node.js applications can leverage OIDC to authenticate users across different domains and organizations. By establishing trust relationships with external identity providers, applications can support federated login, allowing users to authenticate with their existing credentials from providers like Google, Microsoft, or corporate identity systems. This approach simplifies user management and enhances security by centralizing authentication processes.

Security best practices should be followed throughout the OIDC integration process in Node.js applications. This includes using HTTPS for all communications, protecting client secrets, implementing proper error handling, and monitoring authentication events for suspicious activity. Regularly updating dependencies and libraries to address security vulnerabilities is also crucial for maintaining a secure application.

In summary, integrating OpenID Connect into Node.js applications provides a secure, standardized approach to user authentication and identity management. By leveraging libraries like passport-openidconnect and openid-client, developers can implement robust authentication mechanisms, manage tokens securely, and deliver seamless user experiences. OIDC's flexibility and comprehensive security features make it an essential tool for building modern, secure Node.js applications that meet the demands of today's digital landscape.

OIDC in Cloud and SaaS Environments

OpenID Connect (OIDC) has become a cornerstone of secure identity management in cloud and Software-as-a-Service (SaaS) environments. As more organizations migrate their applications and infrastructure to the cloud, the need for standardized, interoperable authentication protocols has grown significantly. OIDC, built on top of the OAuth 2.0 framework, provides a robust solution for managing user identities and securing access across multiple cloud services and SaaS applications. Its widespread adoption is driven by the demand for seamless user experiences, enhanced security, and simplified integration in distributed, multi-tenant environments.

In cloud environments, where applications and services are often distributed across various platforms and providers, OIDC plays a crucial role in enabling Single Sign-On (SSO) and federated identity management. SSO allows users to authenticate once and gain access to multiple cloud services without needing to log in separately to each one. This seamless authentication experience is particularly valuable in enterprise settings, where employees use a variety of SaaS applications, such as Microsoft 365, Google Workspace, Salesforce, and more. By implementing OIDC, organizations can streamline the authentication process, reduce password fatigue, and enhance user productivity.

Federated identity management, facilitated by OIDC, allows organizations to establish trust relationships between different identity providers and service providers. This means that users can authenticate with their organization's identity provider and access third-party cloud services without creating separate accounts. For example, an employee can use their corporate credentials to log in to a SaaS application like Slack or Dropbox, leveraging the OIDC protocol to securely transmit identity information between the identity provider and the service provider. This not only simplifies user management but also centralizes control over authentication policies and security measures.

The integration of OIDC in cloud environments also addresses critical security concerns. By relying on standardized protocols and secure token-based authentication, OIDC helps protect against common threats such as phishing, credential theft, and unauthorized access.

Access tokens and ID tokens issued by the identity provider are cryptographically signed, ensuring their integrity and authenticity. These tokens include claims that convey essential information about the user, such as their unique identifier, roles, and permissions, enabling fine-grained access control and authorization decisions.

Multi-factor authentication (MFA) is another security feature that is easily integrated into OIDC-enabled cloud environments. MFA adds an extra layer of security by requiring users to provide additional verification factors beyond just a password, such as a one-time code sent to their mobile device or biometric authentication. Many cloud identity providers, like Azure Active Directory and Google Identity, offer built-in support for MFA, and OIDC facilitates the seamless integration of these features into SaaS applications and services.

In multi-tenant SaaS environments, where a single instance of an application serves multiple organizations or customer groups, OIDC provides the flexibility needed to manage authentication and identity at scale. Each tenant can be associated with its own identity provider, allowing users to authenticate with their existing credentials while accessing the shared SaaS platform. This approach not only enhances the user experience but also simplifies the management of identity and access policies across different tenant organizations. OIDC's support for dynamic client registration and discovery mechanisms further streamlines the integration process, enabling SaaS providers to onboard new tenants quickly and securely.

Cloud-native architectures, such as microservices and containerized applications, also benefit from OIDC's capabilities. In these environments, services often need to communicate with each other securely, and OIDC tokens can be used to authenticate and authorize inter-service API calls. By issuing and validating tokens for service-to-service communication, OIDC ensures that only trusted services can interact with each other, protecting sensitive data and maintaining the integrity of the application ecosystem. This is particularly important in cloud environments, where services may be deployed across different regions, providers, or hybrid infrastructures.

Another significant advantage of OIDC in cloud and SaaS environments is its support for scalability and high availability.

Identity providers that implement OIDC are designed to handle large volumes of authentication requests, ensuring reliable performance even during peak usage periods. This scalability is critical for SaaS providers and cloud platforms that serve thousands or millions of users. Additionally, OIDC's token-based architecture reduces the need for maintaining long-lived sessions on the server side, improving the scalability and efficiency of cloud applications.

The use of OIDC in cloud environments also supports compliance with industry standards and regulatory requirements. By implementing standardized authentication protocols and secure token management practices, organizations can meet the security and privacy requirements of frameworks such as GDPR, HIPAA, and PCI-DSS. OIDC's support for audit logging and detailed token claims provides transparency into authentication activities, helping organizations demonstrate compliance and respond to security incidents effectively.

While OIDC offers numerous benefits in cloud and SaaS environments, successful implementation requires careful planning and adherence to best practices. This includes securing client credentials, using HTTPS for all communications, validating tokens properly, and implementing robust error handling and monitoring. Organizations should also regularly update their identity provider configurations and libraries to address security vulnerabilities and ensure compatibility with evolving standards.

In summary, OpenID Connect provides a powerful, standardized framework for managing authentication and identity in cloud and SaaS environments. By enabling secure, seamless access to cloud services, supporting federated identity management, and enhancing security through token-based authentication and multi-factor verification, OIDC addresses the critical challenges of modern identity management. As organizations continue to adopt cloud technologies and SaaS solutions, OIDC will remain a vital tool for ensuring secure, scalable, and user-friendly authentication experiences across diverse digital ecosystems.

OIDC in Microservices Architecture

Microservices architecture has transformed the way applications are developed and deployed, offering scalability, flexibility, and resilience. In this architecture, applications are broken down into smaller, loosely coupled services that can be developed, deployed, and scaled independently. However, managing authentication and authorization across these distributed services poses significant challenges. OpenID Connect (OIDC), built on top of the OAuth 2.0 protocol, provides a robust framework for handling these challenges, offering secure, standardized mechanisms for user authentication and inter-service communication.

In a microservices environment, each service often needs to authenticate requests and ensure that they come from legitimate sources. Unlike monolithic applications, where a single authentication mechanism might suffice, microservices require a more distributed approach to authentication. OIDC addresses this need by enabling decentralized authentication while maintaining centralized identity management. This allows individual services to verify identity tokens issued by a trusted identity provider without having to manage user credentials directly.

The core component of OIDC in microservices is the JSON Web Token (JWT). When a user authenticates through an identity provider, they receive an ID token and an access token. These tokens contain claims that provide information about the user and their permissions. Because JWTs are signed by the identity provider, they can be verified by any service in the microservices architecture without needing to communicate with the identity provider each time. This stateless nature of JWTs is particularly advantageous in microservices, where minimizing inter-service communication overhead is critical for performance and scalability.

Implementing OIDC in a microservices architecture begins with setting up a centralized identity provider. This provider is responsible for authenticating users, issuing tokens, and managing user identities. Services within the architecture rely on this provider to validate incoming requests. When a user logs into the application, they are redirected to the identity provider, which handles the authentication process. Upon successful authentication, the identity provider issues tokens that the client can use to access various services.

Each microservice validates the incoming tokens before processing requests. This involves checking the token's signature to ensure it was issued by the trusted identity provider, verifying that the token has not expired, and confirming that the token's audience (aud) and issuer (iss) claims match the expected values. These validation steps are crucial for ensuring that only authenticated and authorized requests are processed.

Role-based access control (RBAC) and attribute-based access control (ABAC) can be effectively implemented using the claims included in OIDC tokens. Claims such as user roles, group memberships, and specific attributes can be used by microservices to enforce fine-grained access control policies. For example, a service handling financial transactions might check for a specific role in the token claims to ensure that only authorized users can initiate payments.

Inter-service communication is another critical aspect of microservices architecture that benefits from OIDC. Services often need to call each other to fulfill a user's request. In such cases, the calling service can use the access token obtained from the identity provider to authenticate itself to the target service. This process, known as service-to-service authentication, ensures that internal API calls are secure and that only authorized services can communicate with each other.

In some cases, a service might need to act on behalf of a user when calling another service. This is where the OAuth 2.0 concept of delegated authorization comes into play. OIDC supports this by allowing services to pass the user's access token when making requests to other services. The receiving service can then validate the token and enforce access control based on the user's permissions. This mechanism is essential for maintaining a consistent security model across the entire microservices architecture.

Token management is a key consideration when implementing OIDC in microservices. Access tokens are typically short-lived to minimize the risk of misuse if they are compromised. When an access token expires, the client can use a refresh token to obtain a new one without requiring the user to re-authenticate. However, refresh tokens introduce additional security risks and should be handled with care. They should be stored securely and used only when necessary to minimize exposure.

For microservices that handle sensitive data or require high levels of security, additional measures such as token binding can be implemented. Token binding ties the token to a specific client or device, preventing it from being used elsewhere even if it is intercepted. This adds an extra layer of security to the authentication process, ensuring that tokens cannot be misused outside their intended context.

Monitoring and logging are essential components of a secure microservices architecture. Each service should log authentication events, token validations, and access control decisions. These logs can be aggregated and analyzed to detect suspicious activity, such as repeated failed authentication attempts or unusual patterns of service-to-service communication. Implementing centralized logging and monitoring solutions helps maintain visibility into the authentication process and supports rapid response to security incidents.

Integrating OIDC with service mesh technologies like Istio can further enhance security and simplify authentication in microservices. Service meshes provide a dedicated infrastructure layer for managing service-to-service communication, including authentication, authorization, and encryption. By leveraging OIDC within a service mesh, organizations can enforce consistent security policies across all services, streamline token validation, and reduce the complexity of managing authentication at the application level.

Scalability is a primary concern in microservices architecture, and OIDC supports this by enabling stateless authentication mechanisms. Since JWTs are self-contained and do not require frequent communication with the identity provider, services can scale horizontally without the need for centralized session management. This stateless nature allows microservices to handle high volumes of authentication requests efficiently, making OIDC a suitable choice for large-scale, distributed applications.

Implementing OIDC in microservices also facilitates compliance with regulatory requirements and industry standards. By providing a standardized framework for identity management and secure authentication, OIDC helps organizations meet the security and privacy requirements of regulations such as GDPR, HIPAA, and PCI-DSS. OIDC's support for multi-factor authentication (MFA), secure token handling, and detailed auditing further enhances compliance efforts.

In federated microservices environments, where services span multiple organizations or domains, OIDC provides a unified authentication model. By establishing trust relationships between different identity providers, services can authenticate users and other services across organizational boundaries. This capability is essential for enabling secure collaboration in ecosystems such as supply chains, partner networks, and multi-tenant platforms.

In summary, OpenID Connect provides a comprehensive solution for managing authentication and authorization in microservices architecture. Its support for stateless authentication, secure token management, and fine-grained access control makes it an ideal choice for securing distributed applications. By leveraging OIDC, organizations can build scalable, secure, and resilient microservices architectures that meet the demands of modern application development and deployment.

Troubleshooting OIDC Authentication Issues

OpenID Connect (OIDC) provides a secure and standardized way to handle authentication, but despite its robustness, developers often encounter issues when implementing or maintaining OIDC-based systems. Troubleshooting OIDC authentication problems requires a clear understanding of the protocol's components, including tokens, endpoints, and the various flows involved in the authentication process. Common issues arise from misconfigurations, token validation errors, network problems, and incompatibilities between clients and identity providers.

One of the most frequent issues encountered is related to misconfigurations in client applications or identity providers. When integrating OIDC, it is critical to ensure that the client ID, client secret, redirect URIs, and scopes are correctly configured in both the application and the identity provider. A mismatch in these values often results in authentication failures. For example, if the redirect URI specified in the application does not exactly match the one registered with the identity provider, the authentication request will be rejected. Developers should double-check these configurations, ensuring they are consistent and correctly formatted.

Another common problem involves incorrect handling of the OIDC discovery document. The discovery document, typically located at /.well-known/openid-configuration, provides essential information about the identity provider's endpoints and supported features. Issues can occur if the application fails to retrieve this document or if the endpoints provided are incorrect. It is important to verify that the application can access the discovery document over a secure HTTPS connection and that the information within it matches the expected configuration.

Token validation errors are another significant source of authentication issues. OIDC relies heavily on JSON Web Tokens (JWTs) for securely transmitting user information. These tokens must be properly validated to ensure their integrity and authenticity. Common validation errors include issues with the token's signature, expiration time, issuer (iss), and audience (aud). If the application does not correctly verify the token's signature using the public keys provided by the identity provider's JSON Web Key Set (JWKS) endpoint, it may accept invalid tokens, posing a security risk. Conversely, overly strict validation rules can cause the application to reject valid tokens. Ensuring that the token's claims are correctly interpreted and that the validation logic aligns with the identity provider's specifications is essential.

Clock skew between the client application and the identity provider can also lead to token validation errors, particularly with the exp (expiration) and nbf (not before) claims. If the system clocks are not synchronized, the application might consider tokens as expired or not yet valid. Using Network Time Protocol (NTP) to synchronize system clocks across all involved servers can help mitigate this issue.

Network issues and connectivity problems are another area to investigate when troubleshooting OIDC authentication failures. If the client application cannot reach the identity provider's authorization, token, or userinfo endpoints, authentication will fail. This can be caused by network misconfigurations, firewall rules, DNS issues, or temporary outages at the identity provider. Verifying network connectivity, ensuring that the correct ports are open, and checking for any rate limits or IP whitelisting requirements from the identity provider are important steps in resolving these issues.

Error messages returned by the identity provider during the authentication process often provide valuable clues for troubleshooting. OIDC defines a standard set of error codes, such as invalid_request, unauthorized_client, invalid_grant, and unsupported_response_type, which indicate specific problems in the authentication flow. Carefully reviewing these error messages, along with any accompanying descriptions, can help pinpoint the cause of the issue. Enabling detailed logging in both the client application and the identity provider can also provide insights into where the authentication process is failing.

In some cases, issues arise from differences in how various identity providers implement the OIDC specification. While OIDC is a standardized protocol, not all providers support every feature or interpret the specifications in exactly the same way. For example, some providers might have unique requirements for scopes, claim formats, or token signing algorithms. Reviewing the identity provider's documentation for any deviations from the standard OIDC behavior can help identify and resolve compatibility issues.

Cross-Origin Resource Sharing (CORS) errors are another common problem, especially in Single Page Applications (SPAs) that interact directly with identity providers from the browser. If the identity provider's CORS policy does not allow requests from the application's domain, authentication requests will be blocked by the browser. Ensuring that the identity provider's CORS configuration includes the application's origin is necessary to enable successful authentication.

Session management issues can also lead to authentication problems, particularly in applications that rely on maintaining user sessions over extended periods. If session tokens expire unexpectedly or are not refreshed correctly, users may be logged out prematurely or encounter errors when attempting to access protected resources. Implementing proper token refresh mechanisms, using refresh tokens where appropriate, and handling token expiration gracefully are key to maintaining a smooth user experience.

In federated identity scenarios, where multiple identity providers are involved, issues can arise from misconfigurations or trust relationships between the providers. Ensuring that each identity provider is correctly configured to recognize and trust tokens issued by the others is critical. Federation metadata, such as SAML assertions or OIDC discovery documents, must be accurately exchanged and configured to establish a secure and reliable authentication process.

Finally, security settings and policies at the identity provider or within the application itself can inadvertently block authentication attempts. For example, strict security policies might prevent certain scopes from being granted, require multi-factor authentication for specific actions, or impose geographic restrictions on login attempts. Reviewing and adjusting these security settings, while balancing security requirements with user convenience, can help resolve authentication issues without compromising security.

In summary, troubleshooting OIDC authentication issues involves a methodical approach to identifying and resolving problems related to configuration, token validation, network connectivity, and interoperability between clients and identity providers. By understanding the components of the OIDC protocol and carefully analyzing error messages, logs, and system configurations, developers can effectively diagnose and address authentication problems, ensuring secure and reliable access for users across diverse applications and environments.

OIDC Error Codes and Handling

OpenID Connect (OIDC) is a widely used identity layer built on top of the OAuth 2.0 protocol, providing secure authentication and identity management for web and mobile applications. While OIDC is designed to streamline and standardize the authentication process, errors can still occur at various stages of the flow. Understanding these errors, their causes, and how to handle them effectively is essential for maintaining secure, reliable applications and delivering a smooth user experience. This chapter delves into common OIDC error codes, what they signify, and best practices for error handling in OIDC implementations.

OIDC errors typically occur during the authorization, token exchange, or token validation phases of the authentication process. Errors can stem from client misconfigurations, user actions, or issues with the identity provider. Regardless of the source, OIDC defines a standardized set of error codes to facilitate clear communication between clients and identity providers, making it easier to diagnose and resolve issues.

One of the most common error codes encountered in OIDC is invalid_request. This error indicates that the request sent to the authorization or token endpoint is malformed or missing required parameters. For example, if the authorization request is missing the client_id, redirect_uri, or scope, the identity provider will return an invalid_request error. To handle this error, developers should ensure that all required parameters are included and correctly formatted. Detailed logging of the outgoing requests can help identify missing or incorrect parameters quickly.

Another frequently encountered error is invalid_client. This error occurs when the client authentication fails, typically due to an incorrect client_id or client_secret. This can happen if the client credentials are misconfigured or have been revoked by the identity provider. When handling invalid_client errors, it is important to verify that the client credentials are correctly configured in the application and that they match the values registered with the identity provider. Additionally, developers should ensure that the credentials are securely stored and not exposed in logs or error messages.

The invalid_grant error is related to issues with the authorization grant, such as an expired or already-used authorization code, an invalid refresh token, or a mismatch between the redirect_uri in the request and the one registered with the identity provider. This error often occurs during the token exchange process when the client attempts to exchange an authorization code for tokens. To handle invalid_grant errors, developers should ensure that authorization codes are used only once, refresh tokens are valid, and redirect URIs are consistent between the client and the identity provider.

When the client requests a scope that the identity provider does not support or that the user has not consented to, an invalid_scope error is returned. This error indicates that the requested scope is either invalid, unknown, or exceeds the scope granted by the resource owner. To address this error, developers should review the scopes requested in the authorization flow and ensure they align with the scopes supported by the identity provider. Providing clear information to users about the requested scopes and why they are needed can also help mitigate consent-related issues.

The unauthorized_client error occurs when the client is not authorized to request an authorization code using the provided method. This can happen if the client is attempting to use an unsupported grant type or if the identity provider has restricted access based on client configuration. To handle this error, developers should verify that the client is registered for the appropriate grant type and that the identity provider's configuration allows the requested flow.

A server_error indicates an issue on the identity provider's side, such as an internal server error or a temporary service outage. These errors are typically outside the client's control, but handling them gracefully is crucial for maintaining a positive user experience. Implementing retry logic with exponential backoff, displaying user-friendly error messages, and providing alternative authentication methods can help mitigate the impact of server-side errors.

The temporarily_unavailable error is similar to server_error but specifically indicates that the authorization server is temporarily unable to handle the request due to maintenance or overload. This error suggests that the issue is transient and will likely resolve itself over time. In this case, clients should implement retry logic and inform users that the service is temporarily unavailable.

Token validation errors are another common source of issues in OIDC implementations. These errors occur when the client fails to validate the ID token or access token received from the identity provider. Common validation errors include invalid_signature, invalid_audience, invalid_issuer, and expired_token. These errors typically indicate that the token was tampered with, issued by an untrusted provider, intended for a different audience, or has expired.

To handle token validation errors effectively, developers should implement robust token validation logic. This includes verifying the token's signature using the identity provider's public key, checking the aud (audience) and iss (issuer) claims to ensure they match the expected values, and confirming that the token has not expired. Using well-maintained libraries and frameworks for token validation can simplify this process and reduce the risk of implementation errors.

User-related errors, such as access_denied, occur when the user denies the authorization request or when the identity provider rejects the user's credentials. Handling these errors involves providing clear feedback to the user, explaining why the request was denied, and offering options to retry or use alternative authentication methods. For example, if a user denies consent to share their profile information, the application should inform them of the implications and allow them to reconsider.

Error handling in OIDC implementations should also consider security best practices. Sensitive information, such as client credentials, tokens, and detailed error messages, should never be exposed in logs or error responses. Instead, logs should capture sufficient detail to diagnose issues without compromising security, and user-facing error messages should be generic and user-friendly.

Monitoring and logging play a critical role in identifying and resolving OIDC errors. Implementing comprehensive logging of authentication flows, including request parameters, response codes, and error messages, can help detect patterns and diagnose issues quickly. Integrating monitoring tools and setting up alerts for frequent or critical errors enables proactive management of authentication issues and ensures the reliability of the authentication system.

In summary, understanding and handling OIDC error codes is essential for building secure, reliable authentication systems. By implementing robust error handling logic, adhering to security best practices, and leveraging monitoring and logging tools, developers can ensure that their OIDC integrations provide a seamless and secure user experience. Addressing errors effectively not only improves the application's reliability but also enhances user trust and satisfaction in the authentication process.

Extending OIDC with Custom Claims

OpenID Connect (OIDC) is a widely adopted identity layer built on top of the OAuth 2.0 protocol, designed to provide secure and standardized user authentication. It leverages JSON Web Tokens (JWTs) to convey identity information between identity providers and client applications. While OIDC defines a set of standard claims such as sub (subject identifier), name, email, and preferred_username, many applications require additional user-specific information to support custom business logic. This is where custom claims come into play, allowing developers to extend OIDC tokens with additional attributes that meet their unique requirements.

Custom claims are additional pieces of information included in ID tokens or access tokens, providing context about the authenticated user or the session. These claims can include anything from user roles and permissions to organizational identifiers or application-specific settings. By embedding custom claims into tokens, applications can make more granular authorization decisions and personalize the user experience based on specific attributes.

The process of extending OIDC with custom claims begins with configuring the identity provider to include these claims in the tokens it issues. Most modern identity providers, such as Autho, Okta, and Azure Active Directory, offer flexible mechanisms for defining and managing custom claims. This typically involves creating rules, policies, or mappings that determine how custom claims are generated and included in tokens.

For example, in Autho, custom claims can be added using rules written in JavaScript. A rule might retrieve user-specific data from a database or an external API and append it to the ID token. The key for a custom claim must be namespaced to avoid collisions with standard claims. A typical custom claim might look like https://example.com/roles, where roles is an array of user roles assigned by the application.

Here's a sample Autho rule to add custom roles to the ID token:

```
function (user, context, callback) {

  const namespace = 'https://example.com/';

  context.idToken[namespace + 'roles'] = user.app_metadata.roles;

  callback(null, user, context);

}
```

In this example, the roles attribute is retrieved from the user's metadata and included in the ID token under a namespaced key. This approach ensures that the custom claim does not conflict with standard OIDC claims.

In Azure Active Directory, custom claims can be added through custom policies in Azure AD B2C or by modifying the manifest of an app registration. Developers can define directory schema extensions to include additional user attributes, which can then be mapped to claims in tokens. Similarly, Okta allows administrators to define custom claims using the Okta Expression Language, which provides powerful capabilities for manipulating user attributes and including them in tokens.

Once custom claims are included in tokens, the client application must be configured to handle and utilize these claims effectively. This involves parsing the ID token or access token and extracting the relevant claims for use in authorization decisions or user interface personalization. For example, a web application might use a roles claim to determine which sections of the application a user can access, while a mobile app might use a preferences claim to customize the user interface based on the user's settings.

In applications that rely on role-based access control (RBAC), custom claims play a crucial role in enforcing authorization policies. By embedding role information directly into the token, applications can quickly and efficiently determine whether a user has the necessary permissions to perform certain actions or access specific resources. This approach reduces the need for frequent database queries to check user roles, improving performance and scalability.

Custom claims can also support attribute-based access control (ABAC), where access decisions are based on a combination of attributes rather than predefined roles. For example, an application might include claims for the user's department, geographic location, or security clearance level, and use these attributes to enforce complex access control policies. This flexibility allows organizations to implement fine-grained authorization mechanisms tailored to their specific needs.

While custom claims offer significant benefits, they must be managed carefully to ensure security and privacy. Sensitive information should not be included in tokens unless it is strictly necessary for the application's functionality. Tokens are often transmitted over networks and stored on client devices, so including sensitive data increases the risk of exposure in the event of a security breach. Developers should adhere to the principle of least privilege, including only the claims that are absolutely necessary for the application's operation.

Additionally, it is important to consider the size of the tokens when adding custom claims. JWTs are transmitted as part of HTTP headers, and excessively large tokens can impact performance, especially in environments with bandwidth constraints or where tokens are passed frequently between services. Developers should optimize the claims included in tokens, avoiding unnecessary data and using compact data structures where possible.

Token encryption and secure transmission are also critical when working with custom claims. While JWTs are signed to ensure their integrity, they are not encrypted by default, meaning that the contents of the token can be read by anyone with access to it. If custom claims include sensitive information, developers should consider using encrypted JWTs (JWE) or transmitting tokens over secure channels such as HTTPS to protect the data from unauthorized access.

Another consideration when using custom claims is token validation. The client application must validate the token's signature to ensure that it was issued by a trusted identity provider and has not been tampered with. It should also check the token's expiration time (exp claim) and ensure that the audience (aud) and issuer (iss) claims match the expected values. Custom claims do not affect the standard validation process, but developers should ensure that any logic based on custom claims is implemented securely and robustly.

Custom claims can also be used to support multi-tenant applications, where a single instance of an application serves multiple organizations or customer groups. In such scenarios, custom claims can include tenant-specific information, such as the organization's identifier or subscription level, allowing the application to differentiate between tenants and enforce tenant-specific policies.

In federated identity scenarios, where users authenticate through external identity providers, custom claims can help bridge the gap between different systems. For example, an application might map claims from an external identity provider to its own custom claims, ensuring consistent identity and access management across federated environments.

In summary, extending OpenID Connect with custom claims provides a powerful mechanism for enhancing user authentication and authorization in modern applications. By carefully defining, managing, and utilizing custom claims, developers can implement flexible, efficient, and secure identity management solutions that meet the unique needs of their applications. Whether supporting role-based access control, personalizing user experiences, or enabling multi-tenant architectures, custom claims play a vital role in the success of OIDC implementations.

OIDC and Multi-Factor Authentication (MFA)

OpenID Connect (OIDC) is a widely adopted authentication protocol that provides a standardized framework for verifying user identities across various applications and services. While OIDC offers robust security through token-based authentication, modern security landscapes demand even stronger measures to protect sensitive information and prevent unauthorized access. Multi-Factor Authentication (MFA) complements OIDC by adding an additional layer of security, ensuring that users must provide multiple forms of verification before gaining access to protected resources. This combination of OIDC and MFA creates a powerful defense against common security threats like phishing, credential theft, and brute-force attacks.

MFA requires users to present at least two different types of credentials from distinct categories: something they know (like a password), something they have (such as a smartphone or hardware token), or something they are (biometric data like fingerprints or facial recognition). By requiring multiple factors, MFA significantly reduces the likelihood that an attacker can gain unauthorized access, even if one factor, such as a password, is compromised. Integrating MFA with OIDC ensures that this enhanced security is applied consistently across all applications and services that rely on OIDC for authentication.

The integration of MFA into OIDC workflows typically occurs at the identity provider level. Identity providers, such as Google Identity, Azure Active Directory, or Okta, offer built-in support for MFA and can enforce it as part of the authentication process. When a user attempts to authenticate, the OIDC flow redirects them to the identity provider, where they are prompted to enter their primary credentials. If MFA is enabled, the identity provider then prompts the user for an additional verification factor. Only after successfully completing both steps does the identity provider issue an ID token and access token, allowing the user to access the requested application.

From a technical perspective, integrating MFA into OIDC flows involves configuring the identity provider to enforce MFA policies and ensuring that the relying party (the application requesting authentication) can handle the additional requirements. The acr (Authentication Context Class Reference) claim in the ID token is commonly used to indicate the level of assurance achieved during authentication. This claim allows relying parties to verify whether MFA was performed and, if necessary, enforce specific authentication requirements. For example, an application handling sensitive financial data might require a high-assurance acr value indicating that MFA was used, while a less sensitive application might accept single-factor authentication.

The flexibility of OIDC allows for various MFA methods to be implemented, depending on the needs of the organization and the capabilities of the identity provider. Common MFA methods include time-based one-time passwords (TOTP) generated by authenticator apps, SMS-based verification codes, push notifications sent to registered devices, and biometric authentication. Each method has its strengths and weaknesses in terms of security, usability, and implementation complexity. For instance, SMS-based MFA is easy to deploy and user-friendly but is susceptible to SIM swapping attacks, while hardware tokens offer robust security but may be cumbersome for users to manage.

When implementing MFA in OIDC, it is essential to consider the user experience. While MFA enhances security, it can also introduce friction into the authentication process. Striking the right balance between security and usability is crucial. Adaptive MFA, also known as risk-based authentication, addresses this challenge by applying MFA selectively based on contextual factors such as the user's location, device, or behavior. For example, if a user logs in from a trusted device and location, the identity provider might allow single-factor authentication. However, if the login attempt comes from an unfamiliar device or a high-risk location, the identity provider can require additional verification steps. This approach enhances security while minimizing inconvenience for users.

OIDC also supports the concept of step-up authentication, which allows applications to request additional authentication factors during a session when accessing more sensitive resources. For example, a user might log in with a single factor to browse general information but be prompted for MFA when attempting to perform a sensitive operation, such as changing account settings or initiating a financial transaction. This dynamic approach to authentication ensures that higher security measures are applied only when necessary, reducing friction while maintaining strong protection for critical actions.

Implementing MFA with OIDC requires careful consideration of token management and session handling. After a user completes MFA, the issued tokens reflect the authentication level achieved. If the user's session needs to be re-evaluated for security purposes, such as after a period of inactivity or when accessing sensitive data, the application can trigger a re-authentication flow by redirecting the user back to the identity provider with a specific prompt parameter. This parameter instructs the identity provider to prompt the user for additional authentication, ensuring that the session remains secure throughout its duration.

Security best practices are essential when integrating MFA with OIDC. Protecting the integrity of tokens, securing communication channels, and ensuring proper validation of the acr claim are critical components of a secure implementation. Developers should also be mindful of potential vulnerabilities in MFA methods, such as phishing attacks targeting one-time passwords or man-in-the-middle attacks intercepting authentication tokens. Employing phishing-resistant MFA methods, such as FIDO2/WebAuthn-based hardware keys, can mitigate these risks and provide a higher level of security.

Organizations must also consider the management and recovery of MFA credentials. Users may lose access to their second factors, such as losing a phone or forgetting a hardware token. Providing secure and user-friendly recovery mechanisms is crucial to maintaining access without compromising security. Recovery options might include backup codes, alternative verification methods, or identity verification through trusted contacts. However, these recovery methods must be carefully designed to prevent social engineering attacks and unauthorized access.

Monitoring and logging are vital for maintaining the security and integrity of MFA implementations in OIDC systems. Identity providers and relying parties should log all authentication attempts, including successful and failed MFA challenges, along with contextual information such as IP addresses, device details, and timestamps. Analyzing these logs helps detect suspicious activity, such as repeated failed MFA attempts, login attempts from unusual locations, or patterns indicative of credential stuffing attacks. Implementing real-time monitoring and alerting systems can enable rapid response to potential security incidents.

The integration of MFA with OIDC also supports compliance with regulatory requirements and industry standards. Many regulations, such as the General Data Protection Regulation (GDPR), the Health Insurance Portability and Accountability Act (HIPAA), and the Payment Card Industry Data Security Standard (PCI-DSS), mandate strong authentication mechanisms to protect sensitive data. By combining OIDC's standardized authentication protocols with MFA, organizations can meet these compliance requirements and demonstrate their commitment to securing user identities and data.

In summary, integrating Multi-Factor Authentication with OpenID Connect enhances the security of authentication processes while maintaining the flexibility and interoperability that OIDC provides. By enforcing additional verification steps, organizations can protect against a wide range of security threats, ensuring that only authorized users gain access to sensitive resources. Through careful implementation, attention to user experience, and adherence to security best practices, OIDC and MFA together form a powerful foundation for secure, scalable, and user-friendly authentication systems.

Privacy and Data Protection in OIDC

OpenID Connect (OIDC) has become the backbone of modern identity management systems, providing a secure, standardized method for authenticating users and transmitting identity information. While OIDC offers powerful tools for streamlining user authentication, it also presents significant privacy and data protection challenges. Managing sensitive user information responsibly is crucial in ensuring compliance with data protection laws and maintaining user trust. This chapter explores how OIDC handles privacy and data protection, the key principles guiding its implementation, and best practices for safeguarding personal data in OIDC-enabled systems.

At its core, OIDC is designed to minimize the exposure of sensitive user information by leveraging the OAuth 2.0 authorization framework. OAuth was originally developed to allow secure, delegated access to resources without exposing user credentials. OIDC builds on this by introducing an identity layer that uses tokens to convey user information in a secure and standardized way. This separation between authentication and authorization is fundamental to protecting user privacy, as it limits the scope of information shared with third-party applications.

One of the key elements in OIDC related to privacy is the use of scopes. Scopes define the level of access that a client application is requesting from the identity provider. The openid scope is mandatory for any OIDC request, as it indicates that the client wants to perform user authentication. Additional scopes, such as profile, email, address, and phone, request access to specific categories of user information. By controlling which scopes are requested and granted, both users and administrators can manage the amount of personal data shared with client applications. This aligns with the principle of data minimization, which is a cornerstone of many privacy regulations, including the General Data Protection Regulation (GDPR).

Another important concept in OIDC is the use of claims. Claims are pieces of information about the user, such as their name, email address, or unique identifier (sub). These claims are included in the ID token or can be retrieved from the UserInfo endpoint. OIDC provides a standardized set of claims, but it also allows for custom claims to be defined, enabling organizations to extend the protocol to meet their specific needs. However, the inclusion of custom claims must be carefully managed to ensure that only necessary information is shared and that sensitive data is protected.

To further enhance privacy, OIDC includes mechanisms for user consent. When a client application requests access to specific scopes, the identity provider typically prompts the user to grant or deny consent. This ensures that users are aware of what information is being requested and can make informed decisions about sharing their data. In environments where user consent is required by law, such as under GDPR, this feature helps organizations comply with legal obligations while fostering transparency and trust with users.

Data protection in OIDC also involves securing the transmission and storage of tokens. Tokens, such as ID tokens and access tokens, carry sensitive information and must be protected from unauthorized access. OIDC mandates the use of secure communication channels, such as HTTPS, to prevent tokens from being intercepted during transmission. Additionally, tokens should be signed and, when necessary, encrypted to ensure their integrity and confidentiality. The JSON Web Signature (JWS) and JSON Web Encryption (JWE) standards provide the cryptographic framework for securing tokens, ensuring that only authorized parties can read or modify their contents.

Token expiration and revocation are critical for maintaining data protection in OIDC systems. Tokens should have short lifespans to reduce the risk of misuse if they are compromised. When a user logs out or revokes consent, the associated tokens should be invalidated to prevent further access to protected resources. OIDC supports the use of refresh tokens for maintaining long-lived sessions, but these tokens must be stored securely and used with caution, as they provide a means to obtain new access tokens without re-authentication.

Another essential aspect of privacy and data protection in OIDC is the handling of the UserInfo endpoint. The UserInfo endpoint allows client applications to retrieve additional user information after authentication. While this can be convenient, it also introduces privacy risks if the endpoint is not properly secured. Access to the UserInfo endpoint should be restricted to authenticated clients with valid access tokens, and the information returned should be limited to the scopes granted by the user. Logging and monitoring access to the UserInfo endpoint can help detect and prevent unauthorized data access.

Anonymization and pseudonymization techniques can also be applied to enhance privacy in OIDC systems. Anonymization involves removing personally identifiable information (PII) from data sets, making it impossible to link the data back to specific individuals. Pseudonymization, on the other hand, replaces PII with pseudonyms, allowing data to be processed without directly identifying individuals, while still enabling re-identification under controlled conditions. These techniques can be useful for minimizing privacy risks when processing user data for analytics, testing, or other purposes that do not require direct identification.

Privacy by design and by default is another key principle in OIDC implementations. Privacy by design involves integrating privacy considerations into the architecture and development of OIDC systems from the outset, rather than treating them as an afterthought. This includes designing systems to collect, process, and store only the minimum necessary data, ensuring robust access controls, and implementing strong encryption and security measures. Privacy by default means that the strictest privacy settings are applied automatically, without requiring users to manually configure them. This ensures that user data is protected even if users do not actively manage their privacy settings.

Compliance with data protection regulations is a fundamental consideration in OIDC implementations. Regulations such as GDPR, the California Consumer Privacy Act (CCPA), and the Health Insurance Portability and Accountability Act (HIPAA) impose strict requirements on how personal data is collected, processed, and stored. OIDC provides tools and frameworks that help organizations meet these requirements, but compliance also requires careful planning and ongoing management. This includes conducting data protection impact assessments (DPIAs), maintaining records of data processing activities, and ensuring that data subjects can exercise their rights, such as the right to access, rectify, or delete their personal data.

Audit logging and monitoring are essential for ensuring data protection in OIDC systems. Logs should capture detailed information about authentication events, token issuance, and data access, providing a comprehensive record of who accessed what data and when. These logs can be used to detect suspicious activity, investigate security incidents, and demonstrate compliance with regulatory requirements. However, care must be taken to protect log data, as it may contain sensitive information. Logs should be encrypted, access-controlled, and retained only as long as necessary for security and compliance purposes.

In federated identity scenarios, where multiple organizations or domains share authentication infrastructure, privacy and data protection become even more complex. OIDC supports federated identity management by enabling trust relationships between identity providers and relying parties. However, sharing identity information across organizational boundaries requires careful governance and clear agreements about data handling practices. Organizations should establish data sharing agreements that specify the types of data shared, the purposes for which it can be used, and the security measures in place to protect it.

In summary, privacy and data protection are integral to the successful implementation of OpenID Connect. By leveraging OIDC's standardized mechanisms for managing user consent, securing tokens, and controlling data access, organizations can build secure, privacy-respecting identity systems. Adhering to best practices in data minimization, secure transmission, and regulatory compliance ensures that user data is protected, fostering trust and confidence in the authentication process. As privacy regulations evolve and user expectations grow, OIDC will continue to play a crucial role in safeguarding personal information in digital identity systems.

Auditing and Logging in OIDC Systems

Auditing and logging are essential components in securing and managing OpenID Connect (OIDC) systems. As OIDC facilitates user authentication and identity management, the integrity of these processes must be ensured through comprehensive logging mechanisms that capture relevant events, user activities, and system interactions. These logs not only provide insights into the system's health and performance but also serve as crucial tools for detecting unauthorized access, investigating security incidents, and ensuring compliance with regulatory standards.

At the core of OIDC systems are authentication events, which must be meticulously logged to maintain a detailed record of user activities. Each authentication attempt, whether successful or failed, should generate a log entry that includes key details such as the timestamp, user identifier, client application, IP address, and the outcome of the attempt. Logging both successful and failed attempts is critical, as a pattern of repeated failures may indicate a brute-force attack or unauthorized access attempts. Additionally, logging the reasons for authentication failures, such as incorrect credentials or expired tokens, can help administrators troubleshoot issues and improve system security.

Beyond authentication events, token issuance and validation processes must also be thoroughly logged. When an OIDC provider issues an ID token or access token, it should record the issuance event, including details about the requesting client, the scopes granted, and the expiration time of the tokens. Similarly, when a client application or resource server validates a token, the validation event should be logged to provide an audit trail of token usage. These logs are vital for tracking how tokens are used within the system and identifying any anomalies, such as tokens being used outside their intended scope or by unauthorized clients.

Session management is another critical area where auditing and logging play a key role. OIDC systems often manage user sessions that persist across multiple interactions with client applications. Logging session creation, updates, and terminations helps maintain a clear picture of user activity within the system. For instance, logs should capture when a user logs in, when their session is refreshed using a refresh token, and when they log out or their session expires. This information is invaluable for monitoring user behavior, identifying suspicious activity, and ensuring that sessions are managed securely.

In federated identity scenarios, where OIDC is used to facilitate authentication across multiple domains or organizations, logging becomes even more important. Federated authentication involves trust relationships between different identity providers and service providers, and maintaining an accurate audit trail of these interactions is crucial for ensuring the integrity of the federated environment. Logs should capture details of federated authentication requests, token exchanges, and any errors or anomalies that occur during the process.

Another important aspect of auditing in OIDC systems is capturing administrative activities and configuration changes. Identity providers often have administrative interfaces where settings related to authentication policies, client registrations, and user management are configured. Logging administrative actions, such as adding or modifying client applications, changing authentication settings, or updating user attributes, helps maintain accountability and ensures that any unauthorized changes can be quickly identified and addressed.

To maximize the effectiveness of auditing and logging in OIDC systems, logs must be securely stored and protected against tampering. Logs should be written to secure, centralized logging systems that provide redundancy and prevent unauthorized access. Implementing write-once, read-many (WORM) storage for logs ensures that they cannot be altered after they are written, preserving the integrity of the audit trail. Additionally, logs should be encrypted both at rest and in transit to protect sensitive information from unauthorized access.

Analyzing and monitoring logs is essential for proactive security management in OIDC systems. Implementing log aggregation and analysis tools, such as Security Information and Event Management (SIEM) systems, enables real-time monitoring of authentication events and system activities. These tools can correlate log entries from multiple sources, identify patterns indicative of security threats, and trigger alerts for suspicious activities. For example, a SIEM system might detect a sudden spike in failed login attempts from a specific IP address, indicating a potential brute-force attack, and alert administrators to take immediate action.

Logs also play a critical role in post-incident investigations and forensic analysis. In the event of a security breach or unauthorized access, detailed logs provide the evidence needed to reconstruct the sequence of events, identify the source of the breach, and determine the extent of the damage. By maintaining comprehensive and accurate logs, organizations can respond more effectively to security incidents, mitigate their impact, and prevent future occurrences.

Compliance with regulatory requirements is another key reason for implementing robust auditing and logging in OIDC systems. Many regulations, such as the General Data Protection Regulation (GDPR), the Health Insurance Portability and Accountability Act (HIPAA), and the Payment Card Industry Data Security Standard (PCI-DSS), mandate the logging of user access and authentication activities. These regulations often require organizations to retain logs for a specified period, ensure their integrity, and provide access to logs during audits. By adhering to these requirements, organizations can demonstrate their commitment to data protection and avoid penalties for non-compliance.

While logging is essential for security and compliance, it must be balanced with privacy considerations. OIDC systems handle sensitive user information, and logs may contain personally identifiable information (PII) such as user IDs, email addresses, and IP addresses. To protect user privacy, organizations should implement data minimization practices, ensuring that logs capture only the information necessary for security and auditing purposes. Anonymizing or pseudonymizing user data in logs, where feasible, can further reduce privacy risks. Additionally, access to logs should be restricted to authorized personnel, and audit trails of log access should be maintained to ensure accountability.

Regular review and maintenance of logging configurations are necessary to ensure that OIDC systems continue to capture relevant and accurate information. As systems evolve, new authentication flows, client applications, and security requirements may be introduced, necessitating updates to logging policies and practices. Periodic audits of the logging infrastructure can help identify gaps, ensure compliance with security policies, and optimize the effectiveness of the logging system.

In complex environments where multiple OIDC providers, client applications, and resource servers are involved, standardizing logging formats and practices can simplify log management and analysis. Using consistent log formats, such as JSON or Common Event Format (CEF), facilitates automated processing and integration with analysis tools. Standardized logging also ensures that logs from different components can be correlated and analyzed effectively, providing a comprehensive view of the authentication landscape.

In summary, auditing and logging are fundamental to the security, compliance, and effective management of OIDC systems. By capturing detailed records of authentication events, token usage, session management, and administrative activities, organizations can monitor system health, detect and respond to security threats, and ensure compliance with regulatory requirements. Implementing secure, comprehensive, and privacy-conscious logging practices is essential for maintaining the integrity and reliability of OIDC-based authentication systems in today's complex digital environments.

OIDC and Regulatory Compliance (GDPR, HIPAA)

OpenID Connect (OIDC) has become a cornerstone in modern identity and access management, providing a secure and standardized protocol for user authentication. As organizations increasingly rely on OIDC to manage user identities, they must also navigate complex regulatory landscapes like the General Data Protection Regulation (GDPR) in the European Union and the Health Insurance Portability and Accountability Act (HIPAA) in the United States. Both regulations impose strict requirements on how personal and sensitive information is collected, processed, and protected. OIDC implementations must therefore be designed not only with security but also with regulatory compliance in mind.

GDPR, which came into effect in 2018, is one of the most comprehensive data protection laws globally, affecting any organization that processes the personal data of EU residents, regardless of where the organization is located. GDPR emphasizes principles such as data minimization, purpose limitation, and user consent. OIDC can support GDPR compliance through its inherent mechanisms for consent management and data minimization. When a user authenticates through an OIDC-enabled system, the application typically requests access to specific scopes, such as email, profile, or address. Each scope represents a category of personal data that the application wishes to access. GDPR requires that users give explicit consent for their data to be processed, and OIDC facilitates this by allowing identity providers to prompt users for consent before granting access to their data.

Data minimization is another core principle of GDPR that aligns well with OIDC's design. OIDC allows applications to request only the information necessary for their functionality by specifying the appropriate scopes and claims. For example, if an application only needs to verify a user's identity, it can request the openid scope without accessing additional personal information. This approach ensures that applications do not collect excessive data, reducing the risk of data breaches and ensuring compliance with GDPR's data minimization requirements.

Transparency and accountability are also central to GDPR, and OIDC can help organizations meet these obligations through robust logging and auditing capabilities. Every authentication event, token issuance, and data access request can be logged, providing a clear record of how personal data is processed. These logs are crucial for demonstrating compliance during audits and for investigating potential data breaches. However, organizations must balance logging with privacy considerations, ensuring that logs do not contain sensitive information and are stored securely.

HIPAA, on the other hand, focuses on the protection of sensitive health information in the United States. It sets stringent requirements for the confidentiality, integrity, and availability of protected health information (PHI). While OIDC itself is not tailored specifically for healthcare, its security features can support HIPAA compliance by providing strong authentication and access controls for systems handling PHI. One of HIPAA's key requirements is ensuring that only authorized individuals can access PHI, and OIDC's token-based authentication system is well-suited for this purpose.

OIDC tokens, such as ID tokens and access tokens, are cryptographically signed to prevent tampering and can be encrypted to ensure confidentiality. This ensures that PHI transmitted during authentication processes remains secure. Moreover, OIDC supports the use of multi-factor authentication (MFA), which adds an additional layer of security by requiring users to provide multiple forms of verification before accessing sensitive data. MFA is particularly important in healthcare settings, where unauthorized access to PHI can have serious consequences.

Access control and auditability are also critical components of HIPAA compliance, and OIDC facilitates both through its support for granular permissions and detailed logging. Access tokens issued by OIDC can include claims that specify the user's roles and permissions, allowing applications to enforce fine-grained access controls. For example, a healthcare application can restrict access to patient records based on the user's role, ensuring that only authorized personnel can view or modify PHI. Additionally, OIDC's logging capabilities enable organizations to maintain a comprehensive audit trail of who accessed what data and when, which is essential for HIPAA compliance.

Data security and breach notification are other areas where OIDC can support regulatory compliance. Both GDPR and HIPAA require organizations to implement strong security measures to protect personal and sensitive data and to notify authorities and affected individuals in the event of a data breach. OIDC helps mitigate the risk of breaches by securing tokens, encrypting communications, and enforcing strict access controls. However, organizations must also have processes in place to detect and respond to security incidents, including monitoring for unauthorized access and analyzing logs for signs of suspicious activity.

Cross-border data transfers present additional challenges for GDPR compliance, as the regulation imposes strict requirements on transferring personal data outside the EU. OIDC systems must ensure that any data transferred to third countries is adequately protected, either through standard contractual clauses, binding corporate rules, or other approved mechanisms. When using cloud-based identity providers or services that operate internationally, organizations must verify that these providers comply with GDPR's data transfer requirements.

Consent management is another critical aspect of both GDPR and HIPAA compliance. While GDPR explicitly requires organizations to obtain and document user consent for processing personal data, HIPAA requires healthcare providers to obtain patient consent for sharing PHI under certain circumstances. OIDC supports consent management by allowing identity providers to prompt users for consent during authentication and by including consent-related information in the tokens issued. Organizations can use this information to track and manage user consent, ensuring that they comply with regulatory requirements.

Data subject rights under GDPR, such as the right to access, rectify, and delete personal data, must also be supported in OIDC implementations. Identity providers and applications must provide mechanisms for users to view and manage their personal information, including the ability to withdraw consent and request data deletion. OIDC's standardized protocols make it easier to implement these features across multiple applications and services, ensuring that organizations can fulfill their obligations to data subjects.

Vendor management and third-party risk are important considerations for both GDPR and HIPAA compliance. Organizations that rely on third-party identity providers or integrate OIDC into their systems must ensure that these providers comply with relevant regulations. This involves conducting due diligence, reviewing data processing agreements, and ensuring that third-party services implement adequate security measures. Regular audits and assessments can help organizations verify that their partners and vendors adhere to regulatory standards.

In the healthcare sector, Business Associate Agreements (BAAs) are a critical component of HIPAA compliance when using third-party services that handle PHI. Organizations must ensure that any OIDC providers or related services that process PHI on their behalf sign a BAA, committing to HIPAA's security and privacy requirements. Similarly, under GDPR, organizations must have data processing agreements in place with any third parties that handle personal data, specifying how data will be processed, secured, and protected.

Employee training and awareness are also essential for ensuring that OIDC implementations comply with GDPR and HIPAA. Employees must understand their responsibilities regarding data protection and be trained on how to use OIDC systems securely. This includes recognizing phishing attempts, managing authentication tokens securely, and following best practices for handling sensitive data. Regular training sessions and awareness programs can help reinforce these practices and reduce the risk of human error leading to data breaches.

In summary, OpenID Connect provides a robust framework for managing user authentication and identity, but its implementation must be carefully aligned with regulatory requirements to ensure compliance with GDPR and HIPAA. By leveraging OIDC's security features, consent mechanisms, and logging capabilities, organizations can protect personal and sensitive data, manage user consent effectively, and maintain comprehensive audit trails. Ensuring compliance requires a holistic approach that combines technical measures with strong policies, vendor management, and employee training, enabling organizations to navigate the complex regulatory landscape while maintaining secure and user-friendly authentication systems.

Migrating from Legacy Authentication to OIDC

As digital systems continue to evolve, organizations face increasing pressure to modernize their authentication frameworks to enhance security, scalability, and user experience. Many enterprises still rely on legacy authentication methods, such as basic authentication, custom token systems, or older protocols like LDAP and Kerberos. While these systems may have served their purposes well in the past, they often lack the flexibility, security, and interoperability required for today's distributed applications and cloud environments. OpenID Connect (OIDC), built on top of OAuth 2.0, offers a modern, standardized approach to authentication that addresses these challenges. Migrating from legacy authentication systems to OIDC is a critical step for organizations seeking to future-proof their identity management strategies.

The first step in migrating from a legacy authentication system to OIDC is to conduct a comprehensive assessment of the existing infrastructure. This involves identifying all applications and services that currently rely on the legacy system, understanding how authentication is handled, and mapping out the dependencies between components. It is essential to determine which applications can be easily adapted to OIDC and which may require significant changes. This assessment also includes evaluating the security posture of the current system, identifying vulnerabilities, and understanding the limitations that OIDC will address.

Once the existing infrastructure has been assessed, the next phase involves selecting an appropriate identity provider (IdP) that supports OIDC. Popular choices include Autho, Okta, Google Identity, Azure Active Directory, and many others. The choice of IdP depends on factors such as the organization's specific requirements, integration capabilities, scalability needs, and compliance with regulatory standards. The selected IdP will serve as the central authority for issuing and validating tokens, managing user identities, and handling authentication flows.

A critical component of the migration process is mapping the legacy authentication workflows to OIDC flows. Legacy systems often use session-based authentication, where user credentials are stored in server-side sessions. In contrast, OIDC relies on token-based authentication, where tokens like ID tokens and access tokens are issued to clients and used to authenticate requests. Understanding how to transition from session management to token management is key. This includes deciding how tokens will be issued, stored, and validated within the new system.

During the migration, it is important to address how user credentials and data will be transitioned to the new system. If the legacy system uses a proprietary method for storing user credentials, a migration strategy must be developed to move these credentials securely to the new IdP. This might involve re-encrypting passwords using more secure hashing algorithms, prompting users to reset their passwords, or federating existing credentials through integration with the legacy system during the initial phases of migration.

Integrating OIDC into existing applications requires modifying authentication logic to support OIDC protocols. This often involves updating login flows to redirect users to the IdP's authorization endpoint, handling the redirection back with an authorization code, and exchanging that code for tokens. Client libraries and SDKs provided by the IdP can simplify this process, offering pre-built methods for initiating authentication requests, handling token responses, and managing user sessions.

An incremental migration approach is often the most effective strategy, allowing organizations to gradually transition applications and users to OIDC without disrupting business operations. This can be achieved by running the legacy and OIDC systems in parallel during the migration period. Applications can be updated one at a time to use OIDC, while others continue to rely on the legacy system. This phased approach minimizes risk, provides opportunities to identify and address issues early, and allows for user feedback and adjustments along the way.

Backward compatibility is another critical consideration during migration. For systems that cannot be immediately updated to support OIDC, bridging solutions such as authentication proxies or middleware can be used. These solutions act as intermediaries, translating OIDC tokens into formats that the legacy system can understand, and vice versa. This allows older applications to continue functioning while the migration progresses.

Security is a primary motivation for migrating to OIDC, and ensuring that the migration itself is secure is paramount. This includes securing token storage, using HTTPS for all communications, validating tokens properly, and implementing multi-factor authentication (MFA) where appropriate. Proper token validation involves checking the token's signature, issuer (iss), audience (aud), and expiration (exp) claims to ensure that the token is legitimate and has not been tampered with.

User experience should also be a key focus during the migration. OIDC offers features such as Single Sign-On (SSO) that can significantly enhance user convenience by allowing users to authenticate once and access multiple applications without repeated logins. Implementing SSO as part of the migration can improve adoption rates and reduce user friction. Additionally, clear communication with users about changes to the authentication process, potential impacts, and how to navigate the new system is essential for a smooth transition.

Testing is a critical phase of the migration process. Thorough testing ensures that the new authentication flows work as expected, tokens are correctly issued and validated, and security vulnerabilities are identified and addressed. Testing should cover a wide range of scenarios, including successful logins, failed authentication attempts, token expiration, and handling of edge cases such as revoked tokens or inactive accounts. Automated testing tools can help streamline this process and ensure consistent, reliable results.

Monitoring and logging play an essential role in both the migration and ongoing operation of OIDC systems. Comprehensive logs of authentication events, token issuances, and user activities provide valuable insights into system performance and security. These logs can be used to detect and respond to potential security threats, troubleshoot issues, and demonstrate compliance with regulatory requirements. Setting up real-time monitoring and alerting systems can further enhance security by providing immediate notifications of suspicious activities.

Post-migration, it is important to decommission the legacy authentication system carefully. This involves ensuring that all applications have been successfully migrated, all dependencies have been addressed, and there are no remaining systems relying on the old infrastructure. Decommissioning should include securely archiving or deleting legacy credentials and configurations to prevent unauthorized access. A final review and audit of the new OIDC system should be conducted to confirm that all security and compliance requirements are met.

Training and support for administrators and users are critical for the long-term success of the migration. Administrators should be trained on managing the new OIDC system, including user management, token handling, and troubleshooting. Users should be provided with resources and support to navigate the new authentication process, including documentation, FAQs, and access to helpdesk support.

Migrating from legacy authentication systems to OIDC is a complex but essential process for organizations seeking to enhance security, improve user experience, and future-proof their identity management infrastructure. By carefully planning and executing the migration, leveraging OIDC's modern features, and prioritizing security and user convenience, organizations can achieve a successful transition and unlock the full benefits of a standardized, scalable authentication framework.

Comparing OIDC with SAML and Other Protocols

OpenID Connect (OIDC), Security Assertion Markup Language (SAML), and other authentication protocols such as OAuth 2.0 are foundational technologies in modern identity and access management systems. Each protocol was designed to address specific needs in securing digital identities and managing access to resources, and understanding their differences is essential for selecting the right solution for a given environment. While they share some common objectives, including secure user authentication and authorization, their underlying architectures, methods of operation, and use cases vary significantly.

OIDC is a relatively recent protocol that extends OAuth 2.0 to provide authentication in addition to authorization. OAuth 2.0 itself is primarily an authorization framework that allows applications to access user resources without exposing credentials, using access tokens to grant permissions. However, OAuth 2.0 does not specify how to authenticate users or how to obtain user identity information, which is where OIDC steps in. OIDC introduces an identity layer on top of OAuth 2.0, providing standardized ways to authenticate users and deliver identity information through ID tokens. These tokens are typically JSON Web Tokens (JWT), which are compact, URL-safe, and easy to parse in modern web environments.

In contrast, SAML is an older protocol that was developed in the early 2000s to address enterprise needs for Single Sign-On (SSO) across organizational boundaries. SAML uses XML-based assertions to communicate authentication and authorization information between an identity provider and a service provider. The protocol operates over a different transport mechanism than OIDC, typically relying on browser redirects and POST bindings to transmit assertions securely. SAML was designed in an era before RESTful APIs became the norm, and its reliance on XML makes it more complex and heavyweight compared to the JSON-based OIDC.

One of the most significant differences between OIDC and SAML lies in their data formats and developer-friendliness. OIDC uses JSON, a lightweight data-interchange format that is easy to read, write, and parse in most modern programming languages. JSON's simplicity makes OIDC highly suitable for web, mobile, and API-driven applications, where quick and efficient data exchange is critical. SAML, on the other hand, uses XML, a more verbose and complex format that requires more processing overhead. XML's strict syntax and schema requirements can introduce additional challenges for developers, especially in environments where speed and efficiency are paramount.

Another key distinction is how each protocol handles tokens and assertions. OIDC uses JWTs for ID tokens, which are digitally signed and can be optionally encrypted. JWTs are self-contained, meaning they include all the information needed to verify the token's authenticity and integrity without requiring a separate call to the identity provider. This stateless nature makes OIDC highly scalable and efficient, particularly in distributed systems and microservices architectures. SAML assertions, however, are typically signed XML documents that may require more complex parsing and validation. While SAML assertions can be stored and reused within a session, they are not as portable or lightweight as JWTs.

From a deployment perspective, OIDC has gained popularity in consumer-facing applications, mobile apps, and APIs due to its compatibility with modern web technologies and its ease of integration. Its support for RESTful APIs and token-based authentication aligns well with the architecture of contemporary applications. SAML, on the other hand, remains prevalent in enterprise environments, particularly for SSO solutions within and between organizations. Many large enterprises continue to rely on SAML for federated identity management, especially in scenarios where legacy systems and applications require compatibility with established authentication standards.

In terms of security features, both OIDC and SAML offer robust mechanisms for ensuring secure authentication and data integrity. OIDC leverages the security features of OAuth 2.0, including token expiration, revocation, and scopes for fine-grained access control. The use of JWTs with strong cryptographic signatures ensures that tokens cannot be tampered with. SAML also provides strong security through digital signatures and encryption of assertions, ensuring that authentication data cannot be intercepted or altered in transit. However, SAML's reliance on browser-based redirects and XML signatures can introduce complexities that may lead to misconfigurations if not properly managed.

Another authentication protocol worth comparing is OAuth 2.0, which serves as the foundation for OIDC. While OAuth 2.0 handles authorization, granting applications permission to access resources on behalf of a user, it does not specify how to authenticate users or provide identity information. OIDC fills this gap by introducing ID tokens and a standardized authentication process. This distinction is crucial: OAuth 2.0 is about authorization, while OIDC is about authentication. Using OAuth 2.0 alone for authentication purposes can lead to security vulnerabilities, as it was not designed with user identity verification in mind.

WS-Federation is another protocol that has been used for federated identity management, particularly in Microsoft-centric environments. Like SAML, WS-Federation relies on XML-based messages and operates over browser redirects. However, it has largely been overshadowed by OIDC due to the latter's simplicity, modern data formats, and compatibility with a broader range of applications and platforms. While WS-Federation may still be in use for specific legacy applications, OIDC is increasingly becoming the preferred choice for new deployments.

When deciding between OIDC and SAML, the choice often comes down to the specific needs of the organization and the nature of the applications being secured. For modern web and mobile applications that require seamless integration with APIs and responsive user experiences, OIDC offers clear advantages in terms of simplicity, performance, and developer support. Its lightweight nature and compatibility with RESTful architectures make it an ideal choice for today's fast-paced development environments.

In enterprise settings where established infrastructure relies on SAML for federated identity management and SSO, maintaining SAML may be the practical choice. Many enterprise applications, especially older ones, are designed to work with SAML, and migrating to OIDC may involve significant effort and resources. However, as more organizations move toward cloud-based services and modern application architectures, the trend is shifting towards OIDC for its flexibility and alignment with contemporary development practices.

Ultimately, both OIDC and SAML have their strengths and are suited to different contexts. Understanding the nuances of each protocol allows organizations to make informed decisions about which technology best meets their security, scalability, and integration requirements. By leveraging the right protocol for the right scenario, organizations can ensure secure, efficient, and user-friendly authentication experiences across their digital ecosystems.

Security Vulnerabilities and Mitigations in OIDC

OpenID Connect (OIDC) is a widely adopted protocol for user authentication, providing a standardized and secure framework built on top of OAuth 2.0. While OIDC enhances the security of authentication processes across web and mobile applications, it is not immune to vulnerabilities. Understanding the potential security risks in OIDC implementations and the strategies to mitigate them is crucial for safeguarding user data and maintaining the integrity of authentication systems.

One of the most common vulnerabilities in OIDC is token leakage. OIDC uses tokens, such as ID tokens and access tokens, to authenticate users and authorize access to resources. If these tokens are exposed through insecure transmission, storage, or logging, attackers can potentially use them to gain unauthorized access. Token leakage can occur through various means, such as storing tokens in insecure local storage in web browsers, exposing tokens in URLs, or transmitting tokens over unencrypted HTTP connections. To mitigate token leakage, tokens should always be transmitted over secure HTTPS connections, stored securely using mechanisms like HTTP-only cookies, and never included in URLs. Additionally, implementing short token lifetimes and using refresh tokens can limit the impact of token compromise.

Another significant vulnerability in OIDC is the risk of token replay attacks. In a replay attack, an attacker intercepts a valid token and reuses it to gain unauthorized access. To prevent this, OIDC supports mechanisms like the use of nonce values in ID tokens. A nonce is a unique, random string generated by the client during the authentication request and included in the ID token by the identity provider. The client verifies the nonce upon receiving the token to ensure that it matches the original request, thus preventing replay attacks. Implementing strict validation of nonce values and other token claims, such as the audience (aud) and issuer (iss), is essential for protecting against token replay.

Cross-Site Request Forgery (CSRF) attacks are another threat to OIDC systems. CSRF attacks occur when an attacker tricks a user into executing unintended actions on a web application where they are authenticated. In the context of OIDC, CSRF can be exploited during the authorization code flow if state parameters are not properly validated. The state parameter is a unique string generated by the client and sent with the authorization request. When the identity provider redirects the user back to the client with the authorization code, the state parameter should be returned and validated to ensure the request originated from the legitimate client. Using strong, unpredictable state values and validating them on return helps mitigate CSRF attacks in OIDC.

Phishing attacks remain a persistent threat in authentication systems, including those using OIDC. Attackers may create fake login pages that mimic legitimate identity providers to steal user credentials. While OIDC cannot directly prevent phishing, it can support mitigations through mechanisms like multi-factor authentication (MFA) and the use of trusted device recognition. Encouraging users to enable MFA adds an additional layer of security, making it more difficult for attackers to gain access even if they obtain the user's primary credentials. Additionally, educating users to recognize legitimate authentication flows and verifying the authenticity of identity provider URLs can reduce the risk of phishing.

Man-in-the-middle (MITM) attacks pose another risk to OIDC implementations, where attackers intercept communications between the client and the identity provider. This can result in token theft or unauthorized access. To mitigate MITM attacks, all communication in OIDC flows must be encrypted using TLS (HTTPS). Clients should also validate the identity provider's SSL certificates to ensure they are connecting to the legitimate server. Implementing certificate pinning, where the client accepts only specific, known certificates, can provide an additional layer of protection against MITM attacks.

Improper implementation of the redirect URI can introduce security vulnerabilities in OIDC systems. The redirect URI is the endpoint where the identity provider sends the authorization code or tokens after authentication. If this URI is not properly validated, attackers can manipulate it to redirect tokens to malicious endpoints. To prevent this, the identity provider should require clients to pre-register redirect URIs and reject any requests with unregistered or mismatched URIs. Using exact matching for redirect URIs, rather than allowing wildcards or partial matches, ensures that tokens are only sent to trusted endpoints.

Authorization code interception is another vulnerability in OIDC, particularly in public clients like mobile or single-page applications. In this attack, an unauthorized party intercepts the authorization code during transmission and uses it to obtain tokens. The Proof Key for Code Exchange (PKCE) extension mitigates this risk by introducing a code verifier and code challenge into the authorization process. The client generates a code verifier, hashes it to create a code challenge, and includes the challenge in the authorization request. When exchanging the authorization code for tokens, the client must provide the original code verifier, which the identity provider verifies against the code challenge. This ensures that even if the authorization code is intercepted, it cannot be exchanged for tokens without the code verifier.

Insecure token storage on client devices is a significant concern, especially in mobile and browser-based applications. Storing tokens in local storage or session storage can expose them to cross-site scripting (XSS) attacks, where malicious scripts inject code into the application to steal tokens. To mitigate this, tokens should be stored in secure, HTTP-only cookies that are inaccessible to JavaScript. Additionally, implementing Content Security Policy (CSP) headers can help prevent the execution of unauthorized scripts and reduce the risk of XSS attacks.

Lack of proper token revocation mechanisms can also expose OIDC systems to security risks. If tokens remain valid even after a user logs out or changes their credentials, attackers with access to these tokens can continue to access resources. Implementing token revocation endpoints and ensuring that clients regularly check the status of tokens can help mitigate this risk. Additionally, short token lifetimes combined with refresh tokens ensure that compromised tokens have limited usability.

Misconfigurations in identity provider settings or client applications are another common source of vulnerabilities in OIDC systems. These can include weak client secrets, overly broad scopes, or improper handling of token validation. Regular security reviews, automated configuration checks, and adherence to best practices are essential to identify and correct misconfigurations before they can be exploited.

Regular monitoring and auditing are vital for detecting and responding to security incidents in OIDC systems. Logging authentication events, token issuances, and API calls provides a comprehensive audit trail that can be analyzed for signs of suspicious activity. Implementing real-time monitoring and alerting systems enables organizations to detect potential breaches and respond quickly to mitigate their impact.

Finally, staying up-to-date with the latest security advisories and patches for OIDC libraries and frameworks is essential for maintaining the security of authentication systems. As new vulnerabilities are discovered, developers must promptly apply updates and patches to ensure their systems remain protected.

In summary, while OpenID Connect offers a robust framework for secure authentication, it is not without vulnerabilities. By understanding common threats such as token leakage, replay attacks, CSRF, and MITM attacks, and implementing best practices for mitigation, organizations can build secure OIDC systems that protect user data and maintain trust. Regular security assessments, proper configuration, and continuous monitoring are key components of a comprehensive security strategy in OIDC implementations.

Performance Optimization in OIDC Systems

OpenID Connect (OIDC) has become a critical protocol for secure and standardized authentication across modern web, mobile, and enterprise applications. While OIDC provides a robust framework for handling identity, its performance directly impacts user experience and system scalability. As authentication is often the first point of interaction between users and applications, ensuring that OIDC systems operate efficiently is essential. Performance optimization in OIDC involves fine-tuning various components, including token management, network communication, server configuration, and caching strategies to reduce latency, improve scalability, and maintain security.

The performance of an OIDC system starts with the identity provider (IdP), which handles user authentication, token issuance, and validation. A well-optimized IdP can manage a high volume of authentication requests with minimal delay. One way to enhance performance at the IdP level is by optimizing token generation and signing processes. Since OIDC relies on JSON Web Tokens (JWTs), which are cryptographically signed to ensure integrity and authenticity, the cryptographic operations involved can be resource-intensive. Using efficient algorithms such as RS256 or ES256, depending on the security requirements, can balance performance and security. Hardware Security Modules (HSMs) or dedicated cryptographic accelerators can further speed up the signing process for high-throughput environments.

Token validation is another critical aspect of OIDC performance. When a client application or resource server receives a token, it must validate its authenticity and claims. This process often involves checking the token's signature against the public key provided by the IdP's JSON Web Key Set (JWKS) endpoint. Frequent network calls to the JWKS endpoint can introduce latency and reduce performance. To mitigate this, implementing local caching of the public keys with periodic refresh intervals can significantly improve token validation times while maintaining security. Additionally, using short-lived tokens with appropriate expiration times reduces the need for constant validation, balancing performance and security.

Network communication between the client, IdP, and resource servers plays a substantial role in OIDC performance. Minimizing the number of round-trips required during the authentication process is crucial for reducing latency. The authorization code flow, while secure, involves multiple steps: the initial authorization request, the exchange of the authorization code for tokens, and subsequent token validation.

Optimizing these steps involves reducing unnecessary redirects, consolidating requests where possible, and ensuring that network connections are fast and reliable. Using persistent HTTP connections and enabling HTTP/2 can improve the efficiency of network communication by reducing connection overhead and allowing multiplexing of multiple requests over a single connection.

Caching is a powerful strategy for optimizing OIDC performance, particularly when dealing with frequently accessed user information and tokens. The UserInfo endpoint, which provides additional user attributes after authentication, can become a bottleneck if accessed repeatedly. Implementing caching strategies at the client or gateway level reduces the need to repeatedly query the UserInfo endpoint, thereby lowering latency and reducing load on the IdP. However, care must be taken to respect token expiration times and ensure that cached data remains current and secure.

Load balancing and horizontal scaling are essential for maintaining performance in large-scale OIDC deployments. As authentication requests grow, distributing the load across multiple IdP instances ensures that no single server becomes a bottleneck. Load balancers can route authentication requests to the least-loaded server, improving response times and system resilience. Additionally, deploying IdP instances in multiple geographic regions reduces latency for users by directing them to the nearest server, enhancing the overall user experience.

Optimizing session management is another key factor in OIDC performance. While OIDC is primarily stateless, managing user sessions efficiently can reduce the frequency of re-authentication and token refresh operations. Implementing session tokens or leveraging browser-based session storage with secure cookies allows applications to maintain user state without frequent server-side checks. However, session data must be managed carefully to avoid security risks such as session hijacking or fixation.

In mobile and single-page applications (SPAs), where performance is even more critical, additional optimization strategies are necessary. Mobile networks often introduce higher latency and lower bandwidth compared to wired connections. Reducing token size by limiting the number of claims included in tokens and using compact serialization formats can help mitigate these limitations. Additionally, leveraging the Proof Key for Code Exchange (PKCE) extension in public clients not only enhances security but also streamlines the authorization process by reducing the complexity of token exchanges.

Security and performance are often seen as opposing forces, but in OIDC systems, they must coexist harmoniously. While optimizing for performance, it is essential not to compromise on security measures such as token encryption, multi-factor authentication (MFA), and proper validation of token claims. For instance, enabling MFA adds an extra step in the authentication process, which can introduce latency. However, this can be optimized by implementing adaptive MFA, where additional verification is only required under specific risk conditions, such as logging in from a new device or an unusual location.

Monitoring and analytics play a vital role in identifying performance bottlenecks and optimizing OIDC systems. Implementing comprehensive logging of authentication events, token issuance, and validation processes provides visibility into system performance. Analyzing these logs can reveal patterns, such as peak usage times, slow response rates, or frequent token validation errors, allowing administrators to fine-tune system configurations accordingly. Real-time monitoring tools can also provide alerts for performance degradation, enabling proactive intervention before issues impact users.

Database performance is another critical factor in OIDC systems, especially when dealing with large user bases. The IdP often relies on databases to store user credentials, session data, and token information. Optimizing database queries, indexing frequently accessed data, and using in-memory databases for session management can reduce latency and improve overall system responsiveness. Additionally, implementing database replication and sharding strategies can distribute the load and enhance scalability.

As organizations increasingly adopt microservices architectures, OIDC performance optimization must extend to inter-service communication. In such environments, services often authenticate API requests using access tokens issued by the IdP. Ensuring that these tokens are efficiently validated and that inter-service calls are optimized for low latency is crucial for maintaining the performance of the entire system. Techniques such as service mesh integration and token introspection caching can help streamline authentication processes in microservices environments.

In hybrid and multi-cloud environments, where services are distributed across different platforms and providers, ensuring consistent OIDC performance can be challenging. Implementing federated identity management with cross-domain trust relationships allows users to authenticate seamlessly across different environments. Optimizing the performance of federated authentication involves reducing the complexity of trust relationships, minimizing the number of intermediate identity providers, and ensuring fast and reliable communication between federated systems.

Finally, continuous improvement is essential for maintaining optimal performance in OIDC systems. As application requirements evolve and user bases grow, regularly reviewing and updating performance optimization strategies ensures that the system remains responsive and secure. This includes staying up-to-date with the latest developments in OIDC standards, adopting new technologies, and refining existing configurations based on real-world performance data.

In summary, performance optimization in OIDC systems is a multifaceted process that involves fine-tuning identity provider configurations, optimizing network communication, implementing caching and load balancing strategies, and ensuring efficient session and token management. By balancing performance with security and continuously monitoring and refining system performance, organizations can deliver fast, reliable, and secure authentication experiences that meet the demands of modern digital environments.

The Future of OpenID Connect and Digital Identity

OpenID Connect (OIDC) has firmly established itself as a leading standard for identity verification and secure user authentication across digital platforms. As technology continues to evolve, so does the landscape of digital identity, driving the need for more robust, flexible, and user-centric authentication solutions. The future of OIDC lies not just in refining its existing mechanisms but in adapting to the dynamic requirements of emerging technologies such as decentralized identity, zero-trust architectures, and advanced privacy frameworks.

As digital ecosystems become increasingly interconnected, the demand for seamless and secure identity management solutions is at an all-time high. OIDC's token-based authentication model, built on the OAuth 2.0 protocol, has proven to be both scalable and efficient for a wide range of applications, from enterprise systems to consumer-facing apps. However, the proliferation of cloud services, microservices architectures, and Internet of Things (IoT) devices presents new challenges in ensuring secure identity management across distributed systems. To meet these challenges, OIDC is evolving to offer greater interoperability and support for complex, multi-domain environments.

Decentralized identity (DID) is one of the most promising frontiers for the evolution of OIDC. DID aims to shift control of identity data from centralized authorities to individuals, giving users more control over their personal information. This concept aligns with the growing emphasis on privacy and data sovereignty, where users manage their identities through cryptographic proofs rather than relying on a single identity provider. OIDC is poised to integrate with decentralized identity frameworks, enabling hybrid models where users can authenticate using both traditional and decentralized credentials. This integration would allow OIDC to maintain its role as a trusted authentication protocol while embracing the principles of decentralization.

Another significant development in the future of OIDC is its alignment with zero-trust security models. Zero-trust architectures operate on the principle that no entity, whether inside or outside an organization's network, should be inherently trusted. Every access request must be verified continuously, and authentication must be dynamic and context-aware. OIDC can support zero-trust principles by providing continuous authentication mechanisms and integrating with contextual factors such as device health, user behavior, and location. The ability to adapt authentication requirements in real-time based on risk assessments will be a key feature in enhancing OIDC's role in secure access management.

Privacy and regulatory compliance will continue to shape the future of OIDC as data protection laws like GDPR and CCPA evolve and new regulations emerge worldwide. OIDC's support for user consent management and granular data access control aligns with these regulatory requirements, but further enhancements will be necessary to address the increasing complexity of privacy regulations. Features such as selective disclosure, where users can share only specific pieces of information without exposing their entire identity, will become more prevalent. OIDC's token structure may evolve to incorporate privacy-preserving technologies like zero-knowledge proofs and anonymous credentials, ensuring that users' personal information remains protected while maintaining the integrity of authentication processes.

Interoperability with other identity protocols will also be a crucial factor in the continued success of OIDC. While OIDC has gained widespread adoption, many legacy systems and enterprise environments still rely on protocols like SAML and WS-Federation. Bridging the gap between these protocols will be essential for organizations looking to modernize their identity infrastructure without disrupting existing systems. Efforts are already underway to create seamless integrations between OIDC and other protocols, enabling hybrid environments where different authentication standards coexist and interoperate efficiently.

The rise of biometric authentication and passwordless login methods is another trend influencing the future of OIDC. Traditional password-based authentication has long been recognized as a weak point in security, often leading to breaches due to poor password practices or phishing attacks. OIDC is well-positioned to support the shift towards passwordless authentication by integrating with biometric data, hardware tokens, and other forms of secure, user-friendly credentials. By leveraging WebAuthn and FIDO2 standards, OIDC can facilitate secure, password-free authentication experiences that enhance both security and user convenience.

As artificial intelligence (AI) and machine learning (ML) technologies advance, they will play an increasingly important role in identity management and authentication. OIDC could incorporate AI-driven risk assessment and anomaly detection to enhance its security capabilities. For instance, AI algorithms can analyze user behavior patterns and detect deviations that may indicate fraudulent activities, triggering additional authentication steps when necessary. This adaptive approach to authentication, powered by AI, will help OIDC remain resilient against evolving security threats.

The future of OIDC also involves addressing the challenges of scalability and performance in large-scale deployments. As the number of connected devices and users grows exponentially, OIDC implementations must ensure that authentication processes remain efficient and responsive. Innovations such as distributed identity providers, edge computing, and optimized token handling mechanisms will be essential in maintaining the performance of OIDC systems in high-demand environments.

In addition to technical advancements, the future of OIDC will be shaped by the broader digital identity ecosystem and the collaboration between industry stakeholders. Open standards and community-driven development have always been at the heart of OIDC's success, and continued collaboration will be key to addressing new challenges and opportunities. Organizations like the OpenID Foundation, which governs the development of OIDC, will play a crucial role in guiding the protocol's evolution and ensuring that it remains responsive to the needs of developers, enterprises, and end-users.

The adoption of OIDC in emerging technologies, such as blockchain and IoT, will further expand its influence in the digital identity landscape. Blockchain technology offers potential for immutable, transparent identity verification processes, and integrating OIDC with blockchain-based identity solutions could enhance the security and trustworthiness of digital interactions. Similarly, as IoT devices proliferate, OIDC will need to adapt to provide secure, scalable authentication for billions of interconnected devices, ensuring that they can authenticate and communicate securely in a decentralized network.

Education and awareness will also be important in driving the future adoption of OIDC. As the protocol becomes more sophisticated and integrates with diverse technologies, it is essential that developers, IT professionals, and decision-makers understand how to implement and manage OIDC effectively. Providing comprehensive documentation, training resources, and best practices will help organizations harness the full potential of OIDC while avoiding common pitfalls and security vulnerabilities.

In the context of global digital transformation, OIDC's role in enabling secure, seamless, and user-centric identity management will continue to grow. The protocol's ability to adapt to new technologies, address evolving security challenges, and comply with regulatory requirements positions it as a cornerstone of the future digital identity landscape. By embracing innovation and fostering collaboration across the industry, OIDC will remain at the forefront of secure authentication and identity verification in an increasingly connected world.

Real-World Case Studies of OIDC Implementation

OpenID Connect (OIDC) has rapidly become the preferred protocol for user authentication and authorization in a wide range of industries. Its flexibility, security, and ease of integration have made it an essential component in modern digital ecosystems, from large enterprises to small startups. Examining real-world case studies of OIDC implementation provides valuable insights into how organizations leverage this protocol to solve complex identity management challenges, enhance security, and streamline user experiences.

One prominent case of OIDC implementation is Google's use of the protocol across its vast suite of services. As one of the key contributors to the development of OIDC, Google integrated it into its authentication systems to provide secure, seamless access for millions of users worldwide. By adopting OIDC, Google enabled Single Sign-On (SSO) capabilities across its platforms, allowing users to authenticate once and gain access to services like Gmail, Google Drive, YouTube, and Google Workspace without repeated logins. This not only improved user convenience but also strengthened security through centralized identity management and robust token-based authentication mechanisms. The implementation also supported multi-factor authentication (MFA), ensuring that even if credentials were compromised, unauthorized access could be prevented.

In the healthcare sector, OIDC has been instrumental in addressing stringent regulatory requirements for protecting patient data. A notable example is the integration of OIDC by Epic Systems, one of the largest electronic health record (EHR) providers in the United States. Epic leveraged OIDC to secure access to patient records and ensure compliance with the Health Insurance Portability and Accountability Act (HIPAA). By implementing OIDC, Epic provided healthcare providers with a secure, standardized method for accessing patient information across different systems and applications. The protocol's support for fine-grained access control allowed organizations to enforce strict permissions based on user roles, ensuring that sensitive data was only accessible to authorized personnel. Additionally, OIDC's auditing capabilities enabled healthcare organizations to maintain detailed logs of access events, supporting regulatory compliance and facilitating forensic investigations in the event of data breaches.

The financial industry has also embraced OIDC to enhance security and improve user authentication experiences. For instance, a leading European bank implemented OIDC as part of its digital transformation strategy to provide customers with secure, seamless access to online banking services. By adopting OIDC, the bank was able to replace legacy authentication systems that relied on outdated protocols like SAML and custom token-based solutions. The transition to OIDC allowed the bank to implement SSO across its digital platforms, including mobile banking apps, online portals, and third-party financial services. The bank also integrated OIDC with its MFA solutions, using biometric authentication and one-time passcodes to strengthen security. The move to OIDC not only improved the user experience by reducing friction during login but also enhanced the bank's ability to detect and respond to security threats through centralized monitoring and logging.

In the education sector, OIDC has played a crucial role in simplifying access to digital learning resources while maintaining strong security standards. The University of California system, which includes multiple campuses and hundreds of thousands of students and staff, implemented OIDC to unify authentication across its various platforms. Prior to adopting OIDC, the university faced challenges with managing multiple authentication systems for different applications, leading to a fragmented user experience and increased administrative overhead. By integrating OIDC, the university was able to provide SSO capabilities, allowing students and faculty to access learning management systems, email, library resources, and administrative tools with a single set of credentials. The implementation also supported federated identity management, enabling seamless collaboration with other institutions and research organizations. OIDC's robust security features ensured that sensitive academic and personal data were protected, while its scalability allowed the system to accommodate the university's growing user base.

E-commerce platforms have also benefited from OIDC's capabilities, particularly in enhancing customer experiences and securing transactions. A major global online retailer implemented OIDC to streamline customer authentication across its web and mobile platforms. Prior to adopting OIDC, the retailer faced issues with managing multiple authentication flows and inconsistent user experiences across different devices. By transitioning to OIDC, the retailer was able to provide a unified authentication experience, allowing customers to log in seamlessly across various channels. The implementation of OIDC also enabled the retailer to integrate third-party identity providers, such as Google and Facebook, allowing customers to use their existing credentials for quick and easy access. This not only improved customer satisfaction but also reduced the barriers to account creation and login, contributing to increased user engagement and sales. The retailer also leveraged OIDC's support for MFA to enhance security during high-value transactions, protecting customers from fraud and unauthorized access.

Government agencies have also turned to OIDC to modernize their authentication systems and improve access to public services. The UK Government Digital Service (GDS) implemented OIDC as part of its GOV.UK Verify program, which aims to provide a secure and user-friendly way for citizens to access government services online. By adopting OIDC, GDS was able to create a federated identity model, allowing multiple certified identity providers to authenticate users while maintaining a consistent and secure user experience. This approach enabled citizens to use a single identity to access a wide range of services, from tax filings and passport applications to healthcare and social benefits. OIDC's robust security features ensured that sensitive personal information was protected, while its standardized protocols facilitated interoperability between different government systems and third-party providers.

In the realm of social media, OIDC has been instrumental in providing secure and convenient authentication for millions of users. LinkedIn, for example, implemented OIDC to support its third-party developer platform, allowing external applications to authenticate users and access their LinkedIn profiles securely. By using OIDC, LinkedIn provided a standardized and secure way for developers to integrate authentication into their applications, enabling features like social login and personalized content delivery. This not only improved the developer experience but also enhanced security by ensuring that user credentials were never shared directly with third-party applications. OIDC's token-based authentication allowed LinkedIn to maintain control over access permissions and revoke tokens if necessary, protecting user data from unauthorized access.

Telecommunications companies have also adopted OIDC to enhance security and streamline customer interactions. A leading telecom provider in Asia implemented OIDC to unify authentication across its customer-facing platforms, including mobile apps, online portals, and in-store services. By adopting OIDC, the provider was able to offer customers a consistent and secure login experience, reducing the need for multiple credentials and improving user satisfaction. The implementation also supported federated identity management, allowing customers to use their credentials from partner organizations and services. OIDC's support for MFA further enhanced security, protecting customer accounts from unauthorized access and fraud.

These real-world case studies highlight the versatility and effectiveness of OIDC in addressing diverse authentication and identity management challenges across various industries. By adopting OIDC, organizations have been able to improve security, streamline user experiences, and support regulatory compliance, demonstrating the protocol's value as a cornerstone of modern digital identity solutions.

OpenID Connect in the Enterprise

OpenID Connect (OIDC) has become an essential protocol for modern enterprise identity and access management systems, offering a flexible, secure, and standardized approach to user authentication. As organizations increasingly adopt cloud-based services, microservices architectures, and hybrid IT environments, the need for a robust and interoperable authentication protocol has never been greater. OIDC, built on top of the OAuth 2.0 framework, provides the tools enterprises need to manage user identities, streamline access across multiple applications, and enhance security while maintaining a seamless user experience.

Enterprises typically operate in complex environments where users must access a diverse range of applications, from on-premises legacy systems to cloud-based services and SaaS applications. Managing authentication across these disparate systems can be challenging, particularly when users require Single Sign-On (SSO) capabilities. OIDC addresses this challenge by providing a unified authentication mechanism that works across different platforms and environments. With OIDC, users can authenticate once with a trusted identity provider and gain access to multiple applications without needing to re-enter credentials, significantly improving productivity and reducing friction.

One of the key benefits of OIDC in the enterprise is its ability to integrate with existing identity management infrastructures. Many organizations already use directory services such as Active Directory or LDAP to manage user identities and permissions. OIDC can be seamlessly integrated with these systems, allowing enterprises to leverage their existing identity stores while extending authentication capabilities to modern applications. Identity providers like Azure Active Directory, Okta, and Ping Identity offer robust support for OIDC, enabling enterprises to unify their identity management strategies across on-premises and cloud environments.

Security is a top priority for enterprises, and OIDC offers several features that enhance the security of authentication processes. By using JSON Web Tokens (JWTs) for ID tokens, OIDC ensures that authentication data is securely transmitted and can be easily validated by client applications. JWTs are digitally signed, preventing tampering and ensuring the integrity of the token's contents. Additionally, OIDC supports advanced security features such as multi-factor authentication (MFA), ensuring that users provide additional verification beyond just a username and password. This is particularly important in enterprise environments where sensitive data and critical systems must be protected from unauthorized access.

Role-based access control (RBAC) and attribute-based access control (ABAC) are common in enterprise security models, and OIDC supports these through its use of claims. Claims are pieces of information about the user, such as their role, department, or security clearance, that are included in the ID token. Enterprises can use these claims to enforce granular access controls, ensuring that users only have access to the resources and data appropriate for their role. This capability enhances both security and compliance, allowing organizations to meet regulatory requirements and protect sensitive information.

Scalability is another critical consideration for enterprises, particularly those with large and distributed workforces. OIDC is designed to scale efficiently, supporting high volumes of authentication requests without compromising performance. The use of stateless tokens reduces the need for frequent communication with the identity provider, allowing applications to validate tokens locally and improve response times. Additionally, OIDC's support for federated identity management enables organizations to establish trust relationships with external identity providers, facilitating secure collaboration with partners, contractors, and other third parties.

In the context of enterprise cloud adoption, OIDC plays a vital role in enabling secure access to cloud-based services and applications. Many SaaS providers, such as Google Workspace, Salesforce, and Microsoft 365, support OIDC for authentication, allowing enterprises to manage user access through their existing identity providers. This simplifies user provisioning and de-provisioning, ensuring that access to cloud services is tightly controlled and aligned with enterprise security policies. Furthermore, OIDC's interoperability with other protocols, such as SAML and WS-Federation, allows enterprises to bridge the gap between modern cloud applications and legacy systems, facilitating a smooth transition to the cloud.

Microservices architectures have become increasingly popular in enterprise application development, offering flexibility, scalability, and resilience. In these environments, secure inter-service communication is essential, and OIDC provides a standardized mechanism for authenticating API requests and managing service-to-service authorization. By issuing access tokens that include specific scopes and claims, OIDC enables fine-grained control over which services can access which resources, enhancing security and minimizing the risk of unauthorized access.

Enterprises must also consider regulatory compliance when implementing authentication systems, particularly in industries such as finance, healthcare, and government. Regulations such as the General Data Protection Regulation (GDPR), the Health Insurance Portability and Accountability Act (HIPAA), and the Sarbanes-Oxley Act (SOX) impose strict requirements on how user data is handled, stored, and protected. OIDC helps enterprises meet these requirements by providing secure, auditable authentication processes and supporting features like consent management and data minimization. The ability to log and audit authentication events ensures that enterprises can demonstrate compliance and respond effectively to security incidents.

Managing user identities and access across multiple systems and environments can be complex, particularly in large enterprises with diverse IT landscapes. OIDC simplifies this process by providing a centralized authentication mechanism that can be extended to various applications and services. This centralization not only improves security by reducing the attack surface but also enhances the user experience by providing a consistent and seamless login process. Users can access the tools and resources they need without being burdened by multiple credentials, while IT administrators can manage access policies and monitor authentication activity from a single platform.

Enterprises also benefit from the flexibility and extensibility of OIDC. The protocol supports custom claims and scopes, allowing organizations to tailor authentication processes to their specific needs. For example, enterprises can define custom attributes related to their business processes, such as project codes or cost centers, and include these in tokens to facilitate access control and reporting. This adaptability makes OIDC a versatile solution that can be customized to fit the unique requirements of different organizations and industries.

The adoption of OIDC in the enterprise also supports digital transformation initiatives, enabling organizations to modernize their IT infrastructure and improve agility. By standardizing authentication processes and integrating with modern development frameworks, OIDC facilitates the development and deployment of new applications and services. This accelerates time-to-market for new products, enhances collaboration across teams, and supports innovation by providing a secure and scalable foundation for digital initiatives.

Finally, as enterprises increasingly adopt hybrid and multi-cloud strategies, OIDC provides the interoperability needed to manage authentication across diverse environments. Whether applications are hosted on-premises, in private clouds, or across multiple public cloud providers, OIDC ensures consistent and secure authentication processes. This flexibility is essential for organizations that need to maintain control over user identities while leveraging the benefits of cloud computing.

In summary, OpenID Connect offers a powerful and flexible solution for enterprise authentication and identity management. Its ability to integrate with existing systems, enhance security, support scalability, and facilitate compliance makes it an ideal choice for organizations navigating the complexities of modern IT environments. By adopting OIDC, enterprises can streamline access management, improve user experiences, and build a secure foundation for digital transformation and innovation.

Contributing to the OIDC Community and Standards

OpenID Connect (OIDC) has become a cornerstone of modern authentication and identity management, providing a secure, standardized protocol that supports a wide range of applications across industries. This success is largely attributed to the vibrant and collaborative community that drives the development and evolution of

OIDC standards. Contributing to the OIDC community is not just about advancing the technology—it's about participating in a global effort to create more secure, interoperable, and user-friendly digital identity solutions. By engaging with the OIDC community, developers, security professionals, and organizations can help shape the future of digital identity, ensuring that it meets the evolving needs of users and enterprises alike.

The OpenID Foundation is the primary body responsible for the development and maintenance of OIDC standards. As a non-profit, international organization, the foundation brings together a diverse group of stakeholders, including technology companies, academic institutions, and individual contributors. The foundation's mission is to promote, protect, and advance the OpenID community and its standards through open collaboration and transparent processes. Members of the OpenID Foundation have the opportunity to participate in working groups, propose new specifications, and contribute to the ongoing development of OIDC.

One of the most impactful ways to contribute to the OIDC community is by participating in working groups. These groups focus on specific aspects of the OIDC protocol, such as security, interoperability, and new feature development. Working groups are composed of experts from various backgrounds who collaborate to draft specifications, review proposals, and address challenges within the protocol. By joining a working group, contributors can share their expertise, learn from others, and play a direct role in shaping the direction of OIDC. Participation in these groups often involves attending regular meetings, contributing to discussions, and reviewing technical documents.

In addition to working groups, the OIDC community thrives on the contributions of developers who build tools, libraries, and implementations that support the protocol. Open-source projects are a critical component of the OIDC ecosystem, providing accessible resources for developers to integrate OIDC into their applications. By contributing code, reporting bugs, or creating documentation for open-source OIDC projects, developers can help improve the quality and usability of the protocol. Platforms like GitHub host many OIDC-related repositories, offering a collaborative environment where contributors can submit pull requests, participate in code reviews, and engage with other developers.

Contributing to the OIDC community also involves sharing knowledge and best practices. Writing blog posts, giving presentations at conferences, and participating in online forums are excellent ways to disseminate information and help others understand how to implement OIDC effectively. Community events, such as the OpenID Foundation's summits and workshops, provide opportunities to connect with other professionals, exchange ideas, and stay informed about the latest developments in OIDC. By sharing real-world experiences and case studies, contributors can provide valuable insights that help others navigate the complexities of OIDC implementation.

Security is a fundamental aspect of OIDC, and contributions to the protocol's security landscape are particularly valuable. Identifying vulnerabilities, proposing security enhancements, and conducting security audits are critical activities that help ensure the robustness of OIDC. The OpenID Foundation operates a security mailing list and a responsible disclosure process for reporting vulnerabilities. By actively engaging in security discussions and contributing to the development of secure practices, contributors help maintain the integrity and trustworthiness of OIDC.

Another important avenue for contributing to the OIDC community is through interoperability testing. Ensuring that different OIDC implementations can work together seamlessly is essential for the protocol's widespread adoption. The OpenID Foundation organizes interoperability events, known as "interop testing," where developers can test their implementations against others to identify and resolve compatibility issues. These events provide a collaborative environment for improving the consistency and reliability of OIDC across different platforms and services.

Organizations also play a crucial role in supporting the OIDC community. By adopting OIDC in their systems and providing feedback on its implementation, organizations help validate the protocol's effectiveness in real-world scenarios. Large-scale deployments can reveal performance bottlenecks, integration challenges, and areas for improvement that might not be apparent in smaller implementations. By sharing these insights with the community, organizations contribute to the continuous refinement and evolution of OIDC standards.

Financial support is another way to contribute to the OIDC community. The OpenID Foundation relies on membership dues and sponsorships to fund its activities, including the development of new specifications, the organization of community events, and the maintenance of essential infrastructure. By becoming a member or sponsor, individuals and organizations can help sustain the foundation's efforts and ensure the continued growth and success of OIDC.

Education and mentorship are vital components of a thriving community, and contributing to these areas helps cultivate the next generation of OIDC experts. Experienced professionals can mentor newcomers, offering guidance on best practices, implementation strategies, and community involvement. Educational resources, such as tutorials, webinars, and online courses, provide accessible entry points for those looking to learn about OIDC. By investing time in teaching and mentoring, contributors help build a knowledgeable and capable community that can drive OIDC forward.

Internationalization and localization are important considerations for making OIDC accessible to a global audience. Contributors can help by translating documentation, ensuring that OIDC implementations support multiple languages, and addressing cultural and regional differences in identity management practices. These efforts help broaden the reach of OIDC, making it a more inclusive and universally applicable standard.

Advocacy and policy engagement are also critical aspects of contributing to the OIDC community. As digital identity becomes increasingly intertwined with legal and regulatory frameworks, it is important for the OIDC community to engage with policymakers and advocate for standards that promote security, privacy, and interoperability. Contributors can participate in public consultations, provide expert testimony, and collaborate with regulatory bodies to ensure that OIDC aligns with emerging legal requirements and supports the broader goals of digital trust and identity governance.

Finally, contributing to the OIDC community is about fostering a spirit of collaboration and mutual support. The success of OIDC is a testament to the collective efforts of a diverse and dedicated community. By working together, sharing knowledge, and supporting one another, contributors help create a resilient and innovative ecosystem that continues to evolve and meet the needs of a rapidly changing digital landscape. Whether through technical contributions, community engagement, or advocacy, every effort helps strengthen the OIDC community and advance the future of digital identity.

Conclusion and Next Steps in OIDC Mastery

Mastering OpenID Connect (OIDC) is not just about understanding its technical specifications but also about appreciating its role in the broader landscape of digital identity and secure authentication. As organizations increasingly move to cloud-based infrastructures, adopt microservices architectures, and embrace hybrid IT environments, OIDC has proven to be a critical tool in managing identities securely and efficiently. Throughout this exploration of OIDC, we have delved into its architecture, token-based mechanisms, security protocols, and real-world applications, gaining a comprehensive understanding of how it empowers modern authentication solutions.

OIDC's strength lies in its simplicity and flexibility. Built on top of the OAuth 2.0 framework, it offers a standardized way to authenticate users and transmit identity information securely across various platforms and services. By leveraging JSON Web Tokens (JWTs), OIDC ensures that identity data is transmitted in a compact, secure, and verifiable format. This has made it the preferred protocol for web applications, mobile apps, and APIs, providing a consistent user experience while maintaining robust security standards. The widespread adoption of OIDC by major identity providers, including Google, Microsoft, and Okta, underscores its significance and reliability in the digital identity space.

While the fundamentals of OIDC are straightforward, achieving true mastery involves understanding its nuances and adapting its capabilities to meet the specific needs of different environments. This includes configuring secure authentication flows, implementing multi-factor authentication (MFA), managing token lifecycles, and integrating with existing identity management systems. It also requires staying informed about evolving security threats and best practices, as the landscape of digital identity is continually changing in response to new challenges and technological advancements.

Security remains a cornerstone of OIDC mastery. Implementing OIDC securely involves more than just following the standard protocol; it requires a proactive approach to identifying potential vulnerabilities and mitigating risks. This includes ensuring secure storage and transmission of tokens, validating token claims rigorously, and using mechanisms like Proof Key for Code Exchange (PKCE) to protect against code interception attacks. Regular audits, security testing, and staying up-to-date with the latest advisories are essential practices for maintaining a secure OIDC implementation. Understanding the broader context of identity threats, such as phishing, token replay attacks, and cross-site request forgery (CSRF), allows practitioners to build more resilient authentication systems.

Beyond technical implementation, OIDC mastery involves integrating the protocol into broader organizational strategies. This includes aligning OIDC with enterprise identity governance frameworks, ensuring compliance with regulatory requirements such as GDPR and HIPAA, and supporting federated identity models that enable seamless collaboration across organizational boundaries. Enterprises must also consider the user experience, balancing security requirements with ease of access to ensure that authentication processes do not become barriers to productivity. By leveraging features like Single Sign-On (SSO) and adaptive authentication, organizations can create secure yet user-friendly environments.

Another important aspect of OIDC mastery is its role in supporting digital transformation initiatives. As organizations modernize their IT infrastructures, migrate to the cloud, and adopt agile development methodologies, OIDC provides the flexibility and scalability needed to manage identities across diverse environments. It enables secure access to cloud services, facilitates the development of secure APIs, and supports the integration of emerging technologies such as IoT and decentralized identity frameworks. By understanding how to leverage OIDC in these contexts, practitioners can drive innovation while maintaining robust security standards.

As the field of digital identity continues to evolve, the future of OIDC will be shaped by emerging trends and technologies. Decentralized identity (DID) is one such trend that promises to give users greater control over their personal information, reducing reliance on centralized identity providers. OIDC is expected to integrate with DID frameworks, enabling hybrid models that combine the strengths of both centralized and decentralized authentication. Similarly, the adoption of passwordless authentication methods, such as biometrics and hardware tokens, will influence how OIDC is implemented, offering new opportunities to enhance security and user convenience.

To stay at the forefront of OIDC developments, continuous learning and engagement with the community are essential. The OpenID Foundation and other industry organizations play a critical role in advancing the protocol, providing resources, and fostering collaboration among developers, security professionals, and identity experts. Participating in forums, attending conferences, and contributing to open-source projects are valuable ways to deepen one's expertise and stay informed about the latest advancements in the field.

For those looking to expand their OIDC knowledge, practical experience is invaluable. Implementing OIDC in real-world projects, experimenting with different configurations, and troubleshooting issues as they arise provides hands-on learning that complements theoretical knowledge. Additionally, exploring advanced topics such as federated identity management, cross-domain authentication, and integrating OIDC with legacy systems can further enhance one's understanding and skills. Collaborating with peers, seeking mentorship from experienced professionals, and sharing knowledge within the community can also accelerate the learning process.

Incorporating OIDC into broader security strategies is another critical step in mastering the protocol. Identity and access management (IAM) is a foundational element of enterprise security, and OIDC plays a central role in enabling secure access to resources. By integrating OIDC with IAM solutions, organizations can enforce consistent security policies, manage user permissions effectively, and monitor access to sensitive data. Understanding how OIDC fits into the larger security ecosystem, including its interactions with other protocols like SAML and OAuth 2.0, is key to building comprehensive and cohesive security frameworks.

As organizations increasingly adopt zero-trust security models, OIDC's role will continue to expand. Zero-trust architectures require continuous verification of user identities and dynamic access controls based on real-time risk assessments. OIDC's token-based authentication and support for contextual information make it well-suited for these environments, enabling adaptive authentication that responds to changing security conditions. Mastering OIDC in the context of zero-trust requires a deep understanding of how to leverage its capabilities to enforce granular access controls and maintain a strong security posture.

In summary, mastering OpenID Connect is an ongoing journey that involves not only understanding its technical specifications but also appreciating its broader implications in the fields of digital identity and cybersecurity. By staying informed about emerging trends, engaging with the community, and continuously refining implementation practices, practitioners can ensure that they are well-equipped to leverage OIDC's full potential. As the digital landscape continues to evolve, OIDC will remain a cornerstone of secure authentication, enabling organizations to build resilient, scalable, and user-friendly identity management solutions that meet the demands of the modern world.